Praise for

FUNERAL BEGINS WITH FUN!

". . . a fantastic memoir, written in a conversational style that is wholly unique. . . . Thompson's totally approachable and friendly voice and clear prose are a sure-fire win for readers to appreciate both the lighter and practical sides of funeral directing, making it an enjoyable and heartening read."

—Asher Syed, for *Readers' Favorite*

"Martin Thompson's storytelling is engaging and often laugh-out-loud funny. . . . a delightful memoir that blends humor, history, and humanity. [His] ability to turn life's most serious moments into opportunities for connection and laughter makes this book a truly memorable read. I highly recommend it."

—Carol Thompson, for *Readers' Favorite*

"*Funeral Begins with Fun!* builds on its catchy title and delivers an unexpectedly humorous account of a normally serious topic. . . . an entertaining and insightful look into a career that went far beyond interacting with the families of the deceased . . . a warm, uplifting, and amusing tale of a life lived to the full."

—Leonard Smuts, for *Readers' Favorite*

Funeral
Begins
with
Fun!

Funeral Begins with Fun!

A FUNERAL DIRECTOR'S HUMOROUS MEMOIR of GROWING UP to RUN the FAMILY BUSINESS— and OTHER TALES from SIX FEET ABOVE

MARTIN THOMPSON

COWTOWN PUBLISHING

Published in 2025 by
Cowtown Publishing

Hardcover ISBN: 979-8-9994220-0-2
Paperback ISBN: 979-8-9994220-1-9
E-ISBN: 979-8-9994220-2-6

Interior design by Stacey Aaronson

Printed in the United States of America

To Janice and Jon,
to the lifelong friends and their families
who made the journey sweeter,
to the incredible people I had the honor to work alongside,
and to the families who trusted me to serve them in their
greatest times of need —
Thank you. You've made this a life worth writing about.

TABLE *of* CONTENTS

INTRODUCTION

Welcome to *Funeral Begins with Fun!*—a title that, in hindsight, probably should've come with a shovel and a warning about dirt under your fingernails. But don't worry—we won't be spending all our time in the graveyard.

You might be wondering, "Why would a funeral director write a book?" Well, after decades in the business, I've learned that humor isn't just a coping mechanism—it's survival. When you spend your days with the dearly departed, you learn to appreciate the absurdity of the living.

At the same time, I love serving families, and I never take their trust lightly. This book is, in many ways, my way of honoring the people who have allowed me into their lives at such a sacred and difficult time. Their trust is the foundation of everything I do.

So, think of this book as a sit-down chat—or maybe a lie-down-and-laugh routine. We'll cover everything from my early days growing up around funeral homes (where "Bring Your Kid to Work Day" had a whole different vibe), to the misadventures of raising kids and pets in a household where "grave" is both an adjective and a noun.

But let's not get too serious—after all, this is a humor book. Or at least, that's the goal. If you find yourself chuckling, then mission accomplished. If you find yourself laughing out loud, then I've done my job. And if you find yourself considering a career in the funeral business—well, I'll let you figure that one out on your own.

So, grab a cup of coffee (or something stronger), settle in, and let's start digging. Who knows? You might just unearth a few laughs along the way.

Part 1

THE EARLY YEARS

BACKYARD BURIALS & CATHOLIC SCHOOL CAPERS

APRIL FOOLS' ARRIVAL:
A TEXAS-SIZED FAMILY HISTORY

A grand entrance on April Fools' Day, a family history as rich as a good Texas barbecue, and a name that thankfully wasn't Thesby.

Let's kick off this journey with a bit of family history that's as colorful as a clown at a funeral (a fitting analogy, considering my line of work).

Picture this: April 1, 1958—a day known for pranks and practical jokes, but also for my grand entrance into this world. Yep, I made my debut at 5:26 a.m. in good ol' Fort Worth, Texas, with my trusty twin sister hot on my heels just five minutes later. We were the fifth and sixth additions to the Thompson clan, courtesy of our parents, Guy and Kathleen Thompson.

Now, when people dig into their ancestry, they usually hope to find out they're descended from royalty or that some great-great-grandfather was a war hero, senator, or secret billionaire. Well, I did—or rather, didn't.

On both sides of my family, we've been workers—farmers, wagon builders, cattlemen, ice cream store owners, movers, milkmen, chicken farmers, and just about everything in between. No presidents, senators, or high-society elites—just good, hardworking folks who kept their heads down and got the job done. And honestly? I wouldn't have it any other way.

I've actually traced the Thompson lineage back more than ten generations, and one thing is clear: we've been here a long time.

My dad, Guy Wilbur Thompson, Jr., was born in Fort Worth to Guy Wilbur Thompson, Sr., a man we affectionately called Daddy Guy. He hailed from Muhlenberg, Kentucky, but for five generations before him, the Thompsons lived in Virginia.

The earliest Thompsons I've found landed just south of Boston—meaning at some point, a distant relative probably had tea near the Boston Harbor (hopefully, not the one tossing it overboard). From there, we migrated down to Virginia, then Kentucky, then Texas—likely chasing better land, better weather, or just running from bad decisions.

One thing's for sure—we liked the names Richard, John, and William. Every generation had at least one of each. I'm just grateful we skipped over my actual grandfather's brothers' names: Thurston, Thexton, and Thesby Thompson.

Can you imagine being called Thesby? I'd never have made it through elementary school.

On my dad's mother's side, we had Eula Richardson Thompson, a Weatherford, Texas, farm girl with a deep family history in the ranching world. I found some pretty interesting tidbits about her family. Nana, as we called her, grew up on a farm where her father was both a farmer and a cattle rancher. But one of the coolest finds? Her dad wrote a firsthand account of his life, which included stories of being a Longhorn cattle rancher in Cisco, Texas. He lost his ranch during a two-year drought, and in a twist of cruel fate, that same land later became part of the Cisco/Eastland Oil Boom of 1919. When someone asked him why he left before the oil boom hit, he simply said: "A man never profits from land that another person leaves for greener pastures."

That, right there, is some Texas wisdom.

And get this—his original log cabin home now sits in the Log Cabin Village in Fort Worth. I never knew that until I was in my 60s. Talk about family history hiding in plain sight!

As for the Richardsons' migration pattern, they followed a pretty classic Texas trajectory:

Massachusetts ➡ Virginia ➡ Kentucky ➡ Missouri ➡ Texas in the mid-1800s.

So, while we weren't rocking crowns or sitting in Congress, we were pioneers, ranchers, and business owners who worked hard and helped build this part of the country.

And that's a history I'm proud of.

So there you have it. A wild mix of assiduous workers, a few questionable name choices, and a grand entrance into this world on April Fools' Day.

Fitting, isn't it? Born into a family full of characters, on a day full of jokes.

Let's just say, from the very beginning—I was destined to have a story to tell.

FROM OHIO TO BACKYARD BURIALS: A FUNERAL DIRECTOR IN THE MAKING

My mother, Kathleen Marie Simon Thompson, made her way from the bustling metropolis of Toledo, Ohio, to not-so-bustling (at the time) Fort Worth, Texas. Her parents, Victor Eugene Simon and Ursula Kelly Simon, were the quintessential Midwest couple—tough, hardworking, and the kind of folks who could weather any storm, including an economic one.

Grampy, as we called him, ran a coal business in Ohio, supplying warmth to homes that actually had a winter (unlike Texas, where we act like the apocalypse is coming when it drops below 40). But then, oil rudely stepped in and put him out of business, forcing a career pivot before career pivots were trendy.

I remember Grampy as the kind of guy who could watch a baseball game on TV while listening to another on the radio—talk about multitasking before it was cool. He and his brothers were apparently quite the ballplayers, with some even making it to the big leagues. But when the coal business crumbled, he packed up and headed south to Texas, where he traded coal for oil field supplies. A classic Texas reinvention story.

Grampy moved to Fort Worth first, leaving Grammy and the kids back in Toledo to finish the school year. He bunked at the Texas Hotel, but homesickness started creeping in. That's when he turned to the Monsignor at St. Patrick's Cathedral, asking if he knew anyone with a room for rent.

And just like that, he ended up renting from my dad.

At the time, Dad had just bought a duplex, living on one side while his parents lived on the other. He and Grampy hit it off immediately, forming a friendship that would accidentally rewrite family history.

Here's the funny part: When Grampy went home to Ohio for Christmas, he invited Dad to come along, with one definite plan: Introduce him to his daughter Terry.

(Spoiler alert: That's not my mom.)

After a few nights of partying with Terry, Dad decided he needed a break. So, who did he end up hanging out with instead?

Her sister: Kathleen.

And just like that, instead of Guy & Terry, it became Guy & Kathleen.

Nice try, Grampy.

Grammy was a proud Irishwoman who had a college degree from Bowling Green University, which wasn't common for women back then. Grampy, on the other hand, hailed from France. So, thanks to them, I ended up with a cocktail of Irish, French, English, and Scottish blood—or as some would say, a mutt with a decent tolerance for whiskey and a love for good bread.

Meanwhile, Dad was running Harveson & Cole Funeral Home, while Mom was juggling the roles of chauffeur, chef, teacher, referee, and all-around keeper of sanity for six kids. We weren't exactly rolling in money, but we also weren't scraping by. What we lacked in luxury, we made up for in a strong Catholic upbringing, a crowded house, and a front-row seat at every funeral we ever attended. In fact, we had a permanent pew at St. Mary's Catholic Church—not because we were special, but because we had no choice.

Some of my earliest memories are a bit fuzzy, but a few stand out:

Kindergarten at Mrs. Massey's—where I probably learned how to color inside the lines, but not much else.

A newspaper photo of me and my twin sister, Martha, on a seesaw at age three—the closest thing we ever got to child stardom.

Mom's famous Christmas card production—which one year involved me playing baby Jesus in a homemade nativity scene. (I peaked early.)

But the real highlight of my childhood was our backyard.

We lived in a sprawling two-story house with a wraparound porch, perfect for watching Texas thunderstorms roll in. My twin sister, Martha, and I were part of a six-kid circus: Cindy, Vic, Teacy, Tim, and us, the twins. Mom and Dad gave everyone creative pet names—except Martha and me. By the time they got to us, they were fresh out of ideas, so we got stuck with our actual names.

That backyard was also where I unknowingly started my funeral director career. Any animal that met its demise within a six-block radius got the full backyard funeral treatment. Birds, squirrels, cats—you name it.

The neighborhood kids would gather, and I'd lead the procession, shoebox coffin in hand. We even had sections for different species—a squirrel section, a bird section, a cat section, and of course, a premium plot for Poochie, our beloved dog.

Poochie was the only one who got a full-metal casket.

(Funeral director foreshadowing? Absolutely.)

Fast forward twenty-five years, and we siblings decided to take a nostalgic trip back to the old house. The new owners were nice folks, and we shared stories of our childhood adventures—

like how we figured out you could drain the bathtub from outside the bathroom (a prank that never got old).

They loved hearing about our antics.

Until we got to the backyard cemetery.

When we casually mentioned that dozens of deceased animals were buried out back, their faces changed.

One week later, the house went on the market.

Oops.

Guess some things are better left buried.

And that, folks, is how I got my start in the funeral business—

Shoebox caskets.

Processions of neighborhood kids.

A backyard cemetery with proper sections.

And a knack for making sure the deceased got a proper send-off.

Who knew a childhood hobby would turn into a lifelong profession?

3

CATHOLIC SCHOOL
SURVIVAL

My education began at Mrs. Massey's Kindergarten School, where I was introduced to the thrilling world of the ABCs, 123s, and the fine art of coloring inside the lines. It was here that my academic struggles—and my twin's academic excellence—made their grand debut.

While Martha soared through lessons with ease and enthusiasm, I gravitated toward more pressing matters—like how to secure a girlfriend before the age of six. Success! I managed to woo a cute little blonde girl I proudly considered my girlfriend. (I may not have excelled at reading yet, but clearly, I was an early adopter of the power of charm.)

That same year, I had my first real memory—one that would shape history.

One early morning, Mom took us to downtown Fort Worth to witness something extraordinary: President Kennedy leaving the Hotel Texas after a breakfast event. If something involved the Church, nuns, or anything remotely Catholic, my mom was guaranteed to be front and center—and JFK was the ultimate Catholic icon.

We saw him off, Then went home to get ready for school. But just as we were about to leave, Mom came in crying. She told us the President had been shot. Even at five years old, I knew this was a terrible thing, though I didn't fully grasp the weight of it.

For the next several days, our television was glued to the Kennedy funeral—a solemn, national tragedy that even a kid like me could feel.

After my stellar performance at Mrs. Massey's (ahem), I was enrolled at St. Mary's Elementary on Magnolia Street in Fort Worth. St. Mary's was run by nuns—and not the friendly, guitar-strumming kind you see in *The Sound of Music*. No, these nuns wore full-length black habits, stiff white wimples, and what I swear were boots built for battle.

They looked serious. And trust me—they were.

To make things even more interesting, the Thompson family had the place surrounded. With siblings in every corner of the school, I was under constant surveillance:

Martha and I were in first grade.

Tim in third.

Teacy in fifth.

Vic in seventh.

Cindy in eighth.

Getting away with anything was impossible. And getting busted at school meant an encore performance at home, so I had twice the motivation to at least *try* to stay out of trouble.

The building itself felt massive, with a cavernous cafeteria in the basement. Years later, when I visited, it seemed a lot smaller—maybe because I had grown, or maybe because Catholic school memories have a way of inflating themselves.

Being a twin came with perks and pains:

Perk: a built-in friend (or at least a reliable witness when you're being falsely accused).

Pain: endless comparisons.

Martha was a straight-A student.

Martha was the teacher's pet.

Martha sat quietly and listened.

Me? I was more of a "free spirit." (That's what you call it when you're not academically inclined but very good at distracting others).

The nuns had a radar for sniffing out troublemakers—and I seemed to be on their watchlist from day one. A good knuckle-rapping with a ruler was practically a daily occurrence. (Deserved? Probably. But still.)

Back in the '60s, there were no fancy diagnoses like ADD or ADHD. If you were smart, you were "gifted." If you struggled, you were "lazy." If you talked too much, you were "disruptive." Unfortunately, I fell into the last two categories.

From first grade onward, school felt like it was written in hieroglyphics.

Studying? A mystery.

Reading? An impossible code to crack.

Test-taking? Rocket science.

Multiple-choice tests became a game of chance. I'd try to break the pattern: "A, B, A, D, D, C . . . ah, what the heck, another C." Effective? No. Did it make me feel like I had a system? Absolutely. And hey, at least I had a 25 percent shot at glory.

Despite my academic struggles, school wasn't all bad. I had good friends. I thrived in PE. And, of course, I developed an early appreciation for the opposite sex.

But lunch? Lunch was a nightmare.

Picture this: a brown paper bag reused so many times that it had more holes than the bag itself. Inside? A sandwich that was 90 percent condiments and 10 percent despair—usually butter and mayo drowning a wafer-thin slice of mystery meat.

The two things I despise most in life? Butter and mayo.

But Mom had a simple rule: "This isn't a restaurant; you'll eat what you're served."

So, what did I do? Into the trash it went, leaving me to survive on chips and chocolate milk. Between tragic lunches and dinners that weren't much better, I managed to graduate high school weighing a whopping 130 pounds. (For context, some ninth graders today outweigh that by 20 pounds more than that.) But hey—who needs extra padding when you've got charm?

Looking back, Catholic school was a character-building experience. It taught me discipline. It kept me humble. And it gave me a healthy respect for nuns, rulers, and cafeteria mysteries.

And as for the academic struggles? Let's say I eventually figured things out—though if life had been multiple choice, I probably would've circled "C" and hoped for the best..

GOLF AND GRIFF

Some people come into your life for a moment, and some stick around forever. I was lucky enough to find a couple of lifelong friends early on, and they've shaped me in ways I'll always be grateful for.

Starting in first grade, I was lucky to have great friends, but one of them stood out above the rest: Jimmy Suarez.

He always saved me a seat.

He always picked me first for baseball and kickball.

He always shared his lunch (which, given my tragic sandwich situation, was a lifesaver).

But the real MVP in my early life wasn't just Jimmy—it was his dad.

My own dad was a master of funeral service, but outdoor adventures, sports, and camping? Not exactly his thing. Jimmy's dad, however, was everyone's second dad. He was my first baseball coach, he took me camping with their family, and—most importantly—he introduced me to golf.

That last one? A game-changer.

I was ten years old when Jimmy told me, "We're going to play golf with my dad." I had no idea what golf was, but we headed to a nine-hole course called Sycamore: a few whiffs, a few topped balls —and then, bam. I connected. The ball soared—probably fifty yards max, but to me? That shot was Tiger Woods–level amazing.

Even though I was a slicer, I was hooked.

Golfing with Jimmy and his dad became a weekly ritual. Before long, he even gave me my first set of clubs: a 3, 5, 7, and 9 iron, a 3-wood, a putter, and a few battered range balls. The clubs weren't new, and they probably weren't even the same brand, but to me, they were gold.

To this day, I can't thank anyone more for giving me something I love than Jimmy's dad. While my dad was perfecting the art of a flawless funeral, Jimmy's dad was perfecting my golf swing. If it weren't for him, I'd probably be a professional kickball player today.

In fourth grade, my parents decided it was time for a change and moved us to the west side of Fort Worth. This meant a new parish, a new school, and saying goodbye to my buddy Jimmy.

Enter Holy Family Catholic School—and with it, Griffin Gunter, my new partner-in-crime.

Griff was legendary for one thing: the backyard fort. And his wasn't just any fort—it was a masterpiece. Think *Swiss Family Robinson*'s treehouse but built by a couple of kids with way too much free time.

Griff's parents, Mr. and Mrs. G, were just as legendary. Mrs. G's lunches? Absolute culinary masterpieces. Mr. G's backyard? The ultimate kid paradise. Griff? The kind of friend who always had your back—literally.

As we got older, bikes became our freedom machines. We rode everywhere. We explored new neighborhoods and pushed the limits of where two wheels could take us.

One day in eighth grade, Griff and I took a long ride and ended up near Z Boaz Golf Course. Out of nowhere, I was hit with the worst stomach cramps of my life. I collapsed. I couldn't ride. I couldn't even sit on my bike. Without hesitation, Griff pushed both bikes back to my house—a several-mile trek.

When we got home, my mom took over. And here's the thing about being sick in the Thompson household: If you got sick, you didn't fake it to stay home. You did everything possible to convince Mom you were fine.

Why?

Because Mom's go-to cure for everything was an enema. And let me tell you, I would've rather suffered in silence. But this time, even I couldn't fake being okay.

The next day, Mom hauled me to the doctor.

Diagnosis? Appendicitis.

Solution? Emergency appendectomy.

And, because my life theme is "Nuns Everywhere," my surgery took place at St. Joseph's Hospital—run by nuns, of course.

Was appendicitis considered major surgery? Some people might say no. I say any surgery done on *me* is major.

But Griff was the real MVP. To this day, I don't remember the pain half as much as I remember him pushing two bikes for miles without a single complaint. That's friendship.

Yes, Griff was my best friend, but we had a whole crew of great guys. Our childhood mischief levels were off the charts:

Shooting at kids with BB guns from Griff's fort.

Papering houses during slumber parties.

Building epic bike jumps in the woods near Ridgmar.

Discovering a friend's dad's *Playboy* collection (for the articles, obviously).

We had no idea that life was about to change.

When grade school ended, we suddenly faced a new challenge—high school. Nolan Catholic brought new friends, new adventures, and new stories. But those childhood years of friendship, mischief, and learning about golf? Those were some of the best times of my life.

And honestly? High school might have brought new friends, but I doubt any of them would've pushed two bikes for me—or shared a Playboy "for the articles."

5

SCOUTING, SURVIVAL,
AND MY ROAD TO THE TOP

W here were we? Ah, yes—my childhood escapades didn't stop at school or backyard funerals. They continued into the wide world of Boy Scouts, where I spent some of my best years under the guidance of Ole Man Gillespie in Troop 32.

Let me set the scene.

My brothers, Vic and Tim, had already blazed the trail before me. Vic made it to Life Scout before discovering girls, which promptly ended his scouting career. Tim, on the other hand, made it all the way to Eagle Scout, setting the bar impossibly high. Me? I was all in.

I officially started my Boy Scout journey at age twelve through Webelos—a fancy title for kids too old for Cub Scouts but not quite full-fledged Boy Scouts. In fourth grade, I earned my Arrow of Light Award, the Webelos' highest honor. In fifth grade, I stepped into Boy Scouts proper and began climbing up the ranks.

Troop 32 was a Knights of Columbus–sponsored troop, meeting in their hall in downtown Fort Worth. Behind the main building was our scout hut, which, in my memory, seemed small—so in reality, it must have been tiny.

At the helm stood Ole Man Gillespie, our scoutmaster with

over forty years of experience. In scouting circles, he was a legend. When we attended campouts with other troops, we strutted with pride because everyone knew Troop 32 and Ole Man.

Our meetings were fun, but the real magic happened on campouts.

Some scout troops were all about campfire songs and marshmallow roasting. Not Troop 32. We were an Eagle Scout machine. Every campout had a mission: earn at least one merit badge or advance a rank. Even after Eagle, there was a push for Palms—Bronze, Silver, and Gold.

We even had our own campground—Camp Murrin—tucked in a perfectly named spot: Whiskey Flats. We pitched our tents along the creek and by the time a weekend ended, I was more mosquito and chigger welts than actual skin.

Of course, the leaders weren't suffering with us. While we wrestled with mystery meat over open flames, Ole Man and his crew had their own section stocked with cases of beer, sardines, and pickled pig's feet (which I refuse to count as food). I suspect steaks were hidden in there, too—though we never got a bite.

One of the most memorable parts of scouting was the Order of the Arrow, the national honor society of scouting. At one Jamboree, they held the "Tap Out" ceremony. All the scouts stood in a line, eyes forward, while the Brotherhood approached silently from behind. If they chose you, they gripped your shoulders and gave the secret taps: three long on the left, one long and two quick on the right.

When I got tapped out, I felt like a king. But that's when the real work began.

Each candidate received a wooden arrow on a cord to hang around his neck. You had to decorate your arrow and complete a strict regimen of tasks. Fail, and you got a notch carved into your arrow. Three notches and you were out.

The final ordeal was a solo campout. You were dropped off alone with your sleeping bag, three matches, and a little food. The rules were simple: build a fire and keep it burning all weekend, make your own meals, and—toughest of all—stay completely silent. Even if someone tried to talk to you, you couldn't respond. For me, that was like asking a baby not to cry.

Sure enough, one afternoon I stumbled across a group of scouts laughing and calling out, doing everything short of juggling to get me to break the rule. I didn't take the bait. Later, when I became part of the Brotherhood, I learned the tricks—and naturally, I used them on the next batch of candidates.

The highlight of every summer was camp. We had two choices: Camp Leonard near Granbury or Worth Ranch near Palo Pinto. My first summer was at Leonard, but from the second year on it was Worth Ranch—a place that, to a young scout, was Mecca.

We had our own campsite there, "Ole Man Campsite," right across from the archery range. It was a hike to the chow hall, the pool, and the river, but that was half the adventure. Canoeing, sailing, and even water skiing was all there.

But the real excitement was in the free time: rattlesnake hunts. We didn't have guns or bows, so we resorted to caveman tactics—stoning the snakes and finishing the job with our trusty pocketknives. By week's end, we'd have more than twenty snakes strung up in camp. The fiercest battle wasn't killing them—it was deciding who got which set of rattlers to take home. Looking back, it sounds like something out of a wilderness survival movie, but at the time it was the height of glory.

One of my best friends from scouting was Chris Guinn. Chris had it all: the newest gear, the sharpest uniform, the kind of hair that could've landed him in a shampoo commercial, and—most importantly—an ice chest full of treasures. While the rest of us lived on charred campfire food, Chris pulled out lunch meat, candy, and once even two bottles of wine (which none of us had a clue what to do with).

Chris wasn't just stylish, he was magnetic. Girls adored him, and you could tell he was headed places. I mostly hung around him for the snacks, but it turned into a lifelong friendship.

In 1972, six of my closest friends, including Chris and me, had our Court of Honor and achieved the rank of Eagle Scout. To this day, it remains one of my proudest accomplishments.

The lessons I learned in Troop 32—leadership, teamwork, resilience—have stayed with me ever since. Whether it was tying knots, building fires, leading younger scouts, or just surviving rattlesnake country with duct-taped tents and paper-thin sleeping bags, every bit of it shaped me.

And while I didn't practice burials for snakes or anything like that, scouting did prepare me for something I never could have imagined back then. Later in life, I had the honor of serving as funeral director for almost all of my scout leaders, including Ole Man himself. His funeral was held at St. Patrick's, packed wall to wall with scouting dignitaries and leaders from across the region. Ole Man had a blanket covered from top to bottom, front and back, with patches from campouts, awards, and achievements spanning decades. St. Patrick's allowed us to use that blanket as his pall, draped with pride over his casket.

Each time I've conducted a funeral for one of those men—my heroes in scouting—it has brought with it a reunion of my scouting friends. Standing with them, remembering those leaders, I've realized how deeply scouting shaped not only my youth but also my calling in funeral service: guiding, honoring, and preserving the legacy of those who meant so much.

That's what Scouting was all about.

INTERLUDE:
PRE-GRADUATION CHRONICLES

B y the time eighth grade graduation was on the horizon, I had already navigated a series of odd jobs, questionable business deals, and a choir audition that I swear was an inside job. But before I get ahead of myself, let's start with the first lesson in my entrepreneurial journey—the art of weeding a playground for pennies on the dollar.

LESSON #1: ALWAYS GET PAID UP FRONT

The summer before seventh grade, Holy Family finally completed a new school building. As part of the improvements, a generous donor funded a fancy new playground. But instead of swings, slides, and monkey bars, this was more of a modern art installation—no grass, just winding concrete sidewalks and bizarre play structures surrounded by gravel. It was basically a weed's paradise.

Enter my first "real" job.

Monsignor Wolf hired me to weed the playground at $1 an hour. Texas summers are as forgiving as a nun with a ruler, so I worked from sun-up until noon before heading to the rectory to see if they needed extra help. Each week, I logged my hours—25, 30, sometimes more. And each week, Monsignor Wolf would say, "Keep track of your hours." What I quickly learned was that this was code for:

"I'll pay you next week."

"Maybe."

"If I feel like it."

By August, I had clocked nearly 300 hours and was dreaming about my sweet $300 payday.

Finally, the big moment arrived. Monsignor strolled over to the collection basket, grabbed five rolls of quarters, and handed them to me.

"Here you go, Martin. I bet you've never seen this much money," he said with a pat on the head.

Wait. WHAT?!

This wasn't $300. This was $50 in quarters. I stood there, clutching the coins, too stunned to argue with a priest.

Lesson learned: always negotiate payment terms in writing.

I took my "fortune" straight to the local convenience store and blew it on buckets of gum. Because nothing says "wise financial decision" like a lifetime supply of chewy sugar nuggets.

LESSON #2: THE DONUT-POWERED PAPER ROUTE

Having tasted the joys of indentured servitude, I figured I needed a new gig. Enter *The Fort Worth Press*, an afternoon newspaper with no Saturday edition and a Sunday morning monster the size of a phone book. My route stretched across Camp Bowie, I-30, Hulen, and Merrick, including some elusive apartment complexes.

Monday through Friday, I'd bike to my paper drop, roll 80 to 100 papers, and make my rounds. But Sunday mornings? Oh, those were a different beast.

I was responsible for hauling 125 papers, each a two- to three-pound behemoth, to two separate drop locations. Carrying that oversized newspaper bag felt like lugging a small refrigerator. So, I hatched a plan. If I had to suffer, why not recruit my friends to suffer with me?

I enticed my neighborhood buddies with the only thing more powerful than money: Dunkin' Donuts hot chocolate and cream-filled donuts. On weekdays, if they pitched in, the payoff was even better—we'd head to Mobley's in Ridglea for root beer floats. That was the kind of luxury you couldn't buy with a paperboy's paycheck.

It worked. We were like a sugar-fueled early-morning gang, roaming the streets before the sun came up. Was it night? Was it morning? Who cared? We had papers to toss and donuts to inhale.

The real challenge, though? Collecting payments.

The houses paid like clockwork. But the apartment folks?

a) wouldn't answer the door;

b) claimed they never ordered the paper; or

c) gave me the classic, "Come back next week."

Meanwhile, I had already paid for those papers out of pocket.

Life lesson #2: Collections are a pain.

LESSON #3: THE BAG BOY BONANZA AT SHADY OAKS

With my paper route earnings dwindling, I needed a new plan. My brother had joined Shady Oaks Country Club and asked me to caddy for him a few times. While there, I noticed guys my age working as bag boys. They got to be around golf all day, they made real money, and, most importantly, there were tips.

So, I applied and Art Hall, the golf pro, hired me. This job paid a whopping $1.25 an hour—plus tips. And the tips were the real magic. Five bucks here—sometimes more if you hustled the bags to the right car fast enough. For a thirteen-year-old, tips meant pocket money, freedom, and the thrill of never knowing what the day might bring.

In other words, it was a game changer that came with a full-day's schedule.

+ 7 a.m. – 10 a.m.: Haul carts up from the barn, load members' clubs, and sprint to their cars to grab their bags (tip potential: high).

+ 10 a.m. – Noon: Free time to hit the range or just horse around.

+ Noon – 2 p.m.: Swap out clubs from morning to afternoon rounds (another tip opportunity).

+ 4 p.m. – Close: Clean clubs, drag the range, and store carts.

And then there was Ben Hogan.

Mr. Hogan was a legend, and he practiced at Shady Oaks a few times a week. When he arrived, whoever was closest to the bag room door got to shag balls for him. I learned to recognize his Cadillac and made sure I was "coincidentally" near the door whenever he pulled in.

The routine went like this: He would dump his shag bag onto the ground. I'd take a damp towel and his shag bag and position myself where he directed. One by one, he'd hit balls—right to my feet. The trick? Catch them on the first bounce, let them spin in the towel to clean themselves, then drop back in the shag bag.

This worked great, as every single iron shot landed at my feet, hit with precision. And at the end? A crisp $5 bill.

That was good money for a thirteen-year-old.

I worked at Shady Oaks until I was eighteen, and to this day, it was one of the best jobs I ever had.

LESSON #4: BEWARE OF SURPRISE ·ERRANDS·

One afternoon, my mom casually told me, "Get in the car, we're running an errand."

I had no idea she was taking me to an audition.

Destination: Texas Boys Choir Headquarters.

Purpose: Apparently, I was about to become a choir boy.

I walked in, clueless, and suddenly, someone called my name. "Sing the National Anthem," they said.

Wait. What?!

So, I sang and clapped back a rhythm they played. Before I knew it, "Congratulations! You're in the Texas Boys Choir!"

IN WHAT?!

Suddenly, I was trapped in a world of daily choir practice, weekend rehearsals, and discipline levels that made the nuns at school seem tame.

One week, my parents left town, and I skipped practice entirely. When they returned, Mom and the choir director showed up at Holy Family and pulled me out of class. Mom said, "If you apologize, you can stay in the choir."

And for the first time in my life, I looked my mom in the eye and said: "No."

I thought she was going to faint. But instead, she just sighed, and that was the end of my very short choir boy career—though at the time, it sure felt like an eternity.

LIFE LESSON #5: BE CAREFUL WHAT YOU CLAP FOR.

Part 2

HIGH SCHOOL DAYS

GOLF, GUTS, AND
GROWING UP

6

GOLF, GUTS, AND GRADUATION

Now that we've covered my grade school days, let's fast forward to high school, where the real fun (and occasional mischief) began. Football games, basketball showdowns, homecoming dances—I wanted to be in the thick of it all. And then, of course, there was golf. Sweet, sweet golf.

Nolan Catholic High School—yep, another Catholic institution— was on the east side of Fort Worth, run by the Diocese, and known for being a college prep school. They fielded teams in everything: football, basketball, baseball, golf, tennis, track, you name it.

Our football program had peaked the year before I showed up. The star then was Horace Ivory, who could score from anywhere on the field—kickoffs, punt returns, running back, even defense. He was a one-man highlight reel who went on to Boston College and then the NFL with the New England Patriots, long before Belichick and his hoodie entered the picture.

By my freshman year, Nolan still had firepower. Mike Dolphin, our quarterback, led us all the way to the state finals. We lost by one heartbreaking point. After that, let's just say the Friday night action was mostly in the stands. By my last three years, you went to the game for a date and some horseplay. A football game might've been happening somewhere down on the field, but it wasn't what we were watching.

Basketball, though—that was another story. Our teams were tough, and my classmate Bobby Forrest could flat-out score. He had a hook shot around the basket that was automatic, one game, racking up over 70 points. We made deep runs in state tournaments, only to fall short at the end.

I still remember one deciding game in San Antonio. We sat in the stands afterward, waiting for the award ceremony. There was a long, awkward delay before they announced they'd *lost the key to the trophy case*. Naturally, the student section erupted. I may have started the chant, but soon the whole gym thundered:

"We've got the key! We've got the key!"

But me? My real home was the golf course. Our team was a mix of some of my best friends:

Mike Hood, our ace golfer and a fellow Eagle Scout from Troop 32.

Phil Shaw, another Troop 32 Eagle Scout (and eventually my brother-in-law).

Barry Corcoran, my neighbor and fellow Sunday paperboy.

Bill Daffcik, another neighbor, always good for a root beer float run.

Randy and Wes Berkowski, brothers with the coolest cars who could somehow always track down beer after—or even during—a round.

And then there was me. I rarely cracked the top five for tournaments thanks to my "homemade swing" (a polite way of saying it looked like I was trying to chop wood instead of hit a ball). But the few times I did make it into the lineup? Unforgettable.

My very first tournament was as a freshman at Lake Arlington Golf Course. Tee time came, and it felt like a football stadium of players was watching. I took my first swing, and *slice!*—the ball ricocheted off a metal trash can ten yards in front of the tee and bounced thirty yards behind me into the gallery. Nothing says "rookie" like walking back past your audience to re-hit.

Another time, at Tenison Park in Dallas, I was paired with senior golfers dipping snuff. When I asked what it was, they generously offered me a sample. "Just tuck it in, suck on it, and swallow—you'll like it," they said. By the ninth hole, I was greener than the fairway, had to withdraw, and spent the afternoon in my car alternating between passing out and puking. Lesson learned.

Thankfully, the rest of my team carried the weight. For three straight years, Nolan's golf team won the state—the only Nolan team to do so at the time. I might've been the weak link, but at least I was part of history.

Of course, high school wasn't just sports. The dances, often after football games, were legendary. By senior year, my old Eagle Scout tentmate Chris and I were heads of the band committee, which meant we had to "scout" potential groups. That required us to check out live music at places like Speakeasy, Electric Circus, I Gotcha, and Spencers.

Now, we couldn't exactly blend in with our Letterman jackets sporting a giant "N." But somehow, beer always found its way to our table.

Our test for a good dance band was simple: could they play "Stairway to Heaven"? If yes, book 'em. At the dances, I always saved that song for my girlfriend, Vicki. It started slow and romantic, then turned into something no human could actually dance to. At that point, I'd lean in: "Alright, Vicki—Coke break?"

Dances usually wrapped up with a late-night stop at Pappa's Pizza, the perfect end to a night of music, laughter, and Letterman jackets reeking faintly of smoke and root beer.

Of course, in between the fun was school itself. Up until then, most of my teachers had been nuns, and I was practically immune to ruler swats. Nolan introduced me to a new breed: the Brothers. Strict, no-nonsense, fiberglass paddle-wielding educators whose mission was to keep guys like me in line.

And Nolan had another twist: "Mods," twenty-minute chunks with three minutes between each, that made up the day. M/W/F classes were two Mods (43 minutes), T/Th classes were three (a brutal 66 minutes). Free time between Mods was supposed to be spent studying in the library or labs. Translation: Nolan gave teenagers unsupervised time and expected miracles. Most of us opted for the Student Center, the parking lot, or the designated smoking areas. (Mine was short-lived—my "mom's" permission slip signature was quickly revoked.)

Still, the Mod system was a golfer's dream. We packed our classes into the morning and had afternoons free to play. With practice rounds, scouting bands, and dances, it's no wonder my GPA never threatened the dean's list. But I did manage to master three survival skills:

1. Do just enough to make the grade.
2. Don't draw too much attention to yourself.
3. And—most importantly—avoid the wrath of those fiber-glass paddles.

Somehow, I made it through Nolan without a single pad-dling—an achievement I wear like a badge of honor. Looking back, I have fond memories of the nuns, the brothers, the games, the dances, the golf team, and even my more "creative" ways of avoiding homework.

That's the Catholic school way—once they get you, you never

really leave. So yes, I graduated. Not with honors, but with plenty of stories, a few slices off the tee, and no paddle marks. I call that a win.

7

EURO ADVENTURES

Our pre-graduation European escapade was a mix of history, art, and, as fate would have it, quite a bit of beer. There were thirteen of us, led by two freshly minted teachers—Miss A and Miss B. They were young, fun, and clearly ready to embrace the chaos of chaperoning a bunch of teenagers.

We flew out of DFW without a hitch, landed in New York, and planned to hop over to Paris. But fate had other plans. Our plane had taken an unexpected detour to Vietnam the night before, which meant it needed extra work. Translation: we were stuck in New York waiting for a replacement.

Eventually, we boarded our flight to Paris, and international airspace became our ticket to underage drinking. With the knowing wink of Miss A and Miss B, we made the most of it.

It turns out that our flight had a few special guests—none other than Ian Anderson and the Jethro Tull band. Yes, the actual Jethro Tull band. I can only imagine their booking agent's nightmare when they landed in Paris:

"Did you realize this was a plane full of high school kids who never stopped asking for autographs?"

I'm sure they tried to fend off with flutes and guitars, but teenagers with Sharpies are relentless.

We landed in Paris at the crack of dawn, checked into the

Orly Hilton, freshened up, and dove headfirst into a whirlwind of museums and cathedrals. After a long day of pretending to soak in culture, we took a barge cruise through Paris—and guess what? No drinking age in Europe either! Our table overflowed with empty bottles of a beer called Star, which became my personal guiding light that night.

On Easter Sunday, we attended Mass at Notre Dame Cathedral, which was awe-inspiring, aside from the constant nuns soliciting donations like they were working on commission. Me? I clung to my francs like they were life support—beer and cigarettes weren't going to buy themselves.

From Paris, we moved on to Brussels, and then to Amsterdam, where I turned seventeen in style. Miss A and Miss B had been given some cash from my parents to throw me a proper birthday celebration. They probably envisioned a nice dinner. Instead, we ended up in a dimly lit bar filled with Heineken and slot machines.

It was all fun and games until we noticed a steady stream of men heading through a door at the back—and never reappearing. One of our crew took a picture, and suddenly we were thrown out faster than a bad poker hand. Only later did we realize we'd accidentally wandered into a brothel.

Oops.

Next stop: Rotterdam.

Two things stood out: tulip fields as far as the eye could see, and the best cheese I'd ever tasted. Naturally, I bought a massive block of it, not realizing that food wasn't allowed on the cruise ship we were about to board for the English Channel crossing.

Cue an impromptu "last supper" style cheese feast before boarding.

Result? A long night of stomach issues and way too many trips to the bathroom. The ship was rocking, and so was I.

Finally, we arrived in London, where we stayed at the Victorian-sounding but slightly dingy Victoriaville Station Hotel. It was a relief to hear English again—or so we thought. We stopped a random Londoner to ask for directions to Westminster Abbey. His response? Pure gibberish. We nodded politely, understanding absolutely nothing.

Almost as bad as Paris. One of our group once tried to ask for the *bathroom* while we were down in the Metro subway system. Over and over, she kept getting the same baffling reply: *"Il n'y a pas de chambres avec baignoire ici dans le métro."* Finally, a Frenchman with a sense of humor took pity on her and explained—she wasn't asking for a restroom at all, she was asking for a *room with a bath*. Lost in Translation, yes.

But London also gave me some of the best memories of the trip. Griff and I managed to score tickets to the original production of *Jesus Christ Superstar*—already my favorite album—performed in a cool, classic London theater. Sitting there, hearing it live, was electric. We almost got tickets to see *Tommy* too—almost. Nearly. Oh well, we tried.

And then there was her. Somewhere between Westminster and *Superstar*, I met what I thought would be my girlfriend for life: long flowing hair, a soft Elkin, North Carolina accent, and a smile that hooked me instantly. Smitten (if that's really a word), I made sure I spent the rest of my trip with her, see ya Griff, and I was seated next to her on the flight back to New York. For a teenager, that was basically destiny.

Back home, graduation day finally arrived. We were asked to write heartfelt quotes for the yearbook. Most people wrote inspirational things about teachers, education, or their bright futures.

Me? I wrote: "The party's over."

Mom was not impressed.

Little did I know, the real adventure was just beginning.

8

NIGHTMAN CHRONICLES

It was January 1, 1976. It had been a completely ordinary night until 9:10 p.m., when Dad strolled into the den with a proposition that would change the course of my life forever.

"You've been itching to work at the funeral home," he said. "Well, I've got a job for you."

"Great, when do I start?"

"Right now. Go relieve your grandmother."

And just like that, I was thrown into the deep end of the funeral business.

My first task after sending Grandma home? Taking over the nightman's post. At seventeen, I had no idea what that meant— but I was about to find out.

I jumped in my car and sped to 702 8th Ave., Harveson & Cole Funeral Home. There was Nana, Eula Mae Thompson, calm as always, waiting with her warm smile. Dad told me to stand at the front door and watch her walk home—a short stroll to the Westchester House where she and Daddy Guy lived.

Quick backstory on my grandparents:

Daddy Guy: small but mighty, a former milkman and butcher at Swift Meat Company, with a garage full of tools for carpentry, mechanics, and yard work.

Nana: the definition of a Southern lady—never smoked, never drank, never cursed. A wizard in the kitchen whose fried chicken and biscuits could've given Cracker Barrel a run for its money.

Dad, on the other hand? If you handed him a hammer, he'd probably embalm it instead of use it.

Once Nana disappeared into the night, I locked the front door. And that's when it hit me: *It's just me. Alone. In this massive, eerily quiet funeral home.*

I called Dad for instructions, and he laid out the nightman's commandments:

+ Go into each stateroom and pick up trash.
+ Check flower water levels with the top knuckle of my finger.
+ Mist the flowers, but not too much—or else, indoor flood.
+ Vacuum if necessary.
+ Turn off most lights but leave one on in any room with an outside window.
+ Head upstairs to the nightman's quarters and wait for the phone to ring.

Most important rule? Answer on the second or third ring—never the first.

Second most important rule? Keep it professional. No "Uh-huh" or "Yeah, sure." Just a crisp, "Harveson & Cole."

The nightman's main job was taking First Calls—when someone passed away. That meant:

Name, location, and time of death.

Doctor's name.

Next of kin and their phone number.

A gentle inquiry about the deceased's size.

Then I'd call the two directors on duty, and they'd come in, make the removal, and embalm immediately.

At 11 p.m., I had completed my checklist and headed upstairs. But to get there, I had to walk through the prep room where the real work happened.

On this particular night, three people were lying there in various stages of care. At seventeen, alone, that was more than enough to test my courage.

My first thought? *What are you going to do if one of them grabs you?!*

I froze. Then I thought, *Martin, if you can't walk through here tonight, you'll never be able to walk through here again.* So, I took a deep breath, walked through, and even patted one on the shoulder, saying: "Good night."

I still do this to this day.

The nightman's quarters were simple: one twin bed, one nightstand with a phone and lamp, one 12-inch black-and-white TV with rabbit ears. The mattress smelled like every bit of its forty years. Cozy wasn't the word—but it was mine.

Now, this is where Mike comes in—my twin sister Martha's fiancé. She thought he should see what funeral home life was like. So, one night, I let him shadow me.

Big mistake.

Mike was nervous from the start, and at 2 a.m., he woke me up, whispering that he needed the bathroom. The only one was at the far end—past a maze of casket selection rooms.

Naturally, the only light switch was at the far end, and I walked him there, turned the lights on, and waited. When he came out, the lights had "mysteriously" turned off.

That's when I positioned myself under a casket.

"Martin? Martin?" Mike whispered, inching forward.

The second his legs were in range, I grabbed one.

BOOM.

Mike shot three feet in the air, bolted down the stairs, and out the back door. Next thing I knew, his tires were squealing across the parking lot.

That was Mike's first—and last—night in the funeral business.

And that, my friends, was how I began my career at the family funeral home: night shifts, creepy prep rooms, and one terrified almost-brother-in-law.

At the time, I didn't know this job would shape the rest of my life. Looking back, though? I wouldn't have had it any other way.

9

THE PATH LESS FOLLOWED:
COLLEGE CHOICES

So, I'd graduated high school, and it was time to choose a college. Now, let's get one thing straight—I was never exactly an academic overachiever. But still, there were two clear paths laid before me:

1) Follow in my brother Tim's footsteps and head to the Seminary in Rome. (My mother's personal favorite option. If you knew my mother, you knew she was devoutly Catholic—as in, first in line for every Mass, Catholic convention, and Pope-related event.); or

2) Follow in my brother Vic's footsteps and go to Texas Wesleyan College (TWC). (Texas Wesleyan, affectionately called Teeny Weeny College, was a small school in Fort Worth not too far from Nolan High School or from Harveson & Cole.)

I'll admit, the idea of Rome had its perks—my brother Tim was over there speaking Italian, wearing the collar, sipping espresso, and eating pasta in piazzas. Not a bad life. But when I stacked it up against country club dates, a little dancing and romance, sneaking in rounds of golf, and topping it off with root beer floats at Mobley Ridglea? Well, let's just say the Vatican lost out to Ridglea's ice cream machine.

To say Mom was disappointed that I didn't go the priesthood route is an understatement. She and our pastor, Msgr. Wolf had been pushing hard for it—probably banking on my weak resistance to authority. But when I chose Wesleyan instead, she kind of just shrugged it off—about like the time I told her I wasn't apologizing to the Texas Boys Choir. (She had practice at being disappointed in me by then.)

But my girlfriend? Yeah, she was NOT on board with the priest plan either. For the good of the Catholic Church (and, let's be honest, my relationship), I chose Wesleyan.

Now, getting into Texas Wesleyan was a mystery to some, including my high school counselor, Dr. Drollinger. She had fancy aptitude tests and data-driven charts that supposedly predicted the future. After my test, which I loved about as much as a root canal, she called me into her office. Her professional analysis? I had about a 1 percent chance of getting into college. And IF, by some divine intervention, I got in . . . I had a 1 percent chance of actually graduating.

Her suggestion? "You should probably look into a career in something sports related."

Now, I wasn't exactly thrilled with the grim educational forecast she gave me. But being great at taking advice, I did the exact opposite and enrolled at Texas Wesleyan.

TWC wasn't your typical massive state university experience. There were no 300-person lecture halls, no frat row filled with weekend keg parties, no getting lost on campus (because the entire campus was roughly the size of a shopping mall). But what we did have? A tight-knit community where you actually got to know your professors; small classes, where skipping was noticed immediately; and, most importantly, a school close enough that I could keep working at the funeral home, which was fine because I wasn't the kind of student who spent all day on campus.

By day: I went to class, trying to prove Dr. Drollinger's 1 percent odds wrong. By night: I was still pulling nightman shifts at Harveson & Cole. By the weekend, I was squeezing in golf whenever possible.

And somehow, despite my counselor's bleak predictions . . . I made it through. One class, one semester, one funeral shift at a time.

Looking back, would the priesthood have been a great choice? For somebody else—absolutely. For me? I think God had different plans. I had a lot more to learn about life, family, and running a funeral home.

So, Dr. Drollinger, if you're reading this? Turns out I had at least a 2 percent chance after all.

10

FROM TEXAS
TO BOSTON

After making it through kindergarten, grade school, high school, and college—a feat I'd been told had a slim-to-none chance of happening—you'd think my school days were finally over. Nope. There was still one more academic hurdle to clear: Mortuary Science School, the final stop on the road to becoming a licensed funeral director and embalmer.

Choosing a mortuary school should have been easy. My brother Vic had gone to the Dallas Institute of Mortuary Science (DIMS), so following in his footsteps seemed like a no-brainer. But, in true Thompson fashion, Dad and I decided to overcomplicate things.

I was engaged at the time, so we figured, why not attend school somewhere exciting? Boston and Pittsburgh both had reputable mortuary schools, and I could work at local funeral homes to gain experience from a fresh perspective. Plus, I thought I might come back with a Boston accent (pahk the cah) or sprinkle in some Pittsburgh slang (yinz guys going to the Steelers game?). So, we embarked on two scouting trips—equal parts career planning and cultural field trip.

Our first stop was Boston, home to the oldest mortuary science school in the country. We scouted four funeral homes where I could potentially work:

+ Waterman's – The crème de la crème of Boston's funeral homes, handling the who's who of Boston society. They were members of the National Selected Morticians (NSM), just like us, which gave them that extra layer of prestige.

+ O'Brien's – An Irish Catholic funeral home with a staircase so grand it looked like it could take you straight to heaven.

+ Ruggerio – The Italian funeral home of Boston, where warmth and tradition were baked in like Sunday gravy.

+ Solomon & Schlossberg – A Jewish Orthodox funeral home that fascinated me most. Everything was wooden— no metal anywhere. The prep tables, the casket rollers, even the water supply came from vats on the roof that collected rainwater, all in accordance with Jewish law. And the kicker? They handled 2,000 calls a year. It was less a funeral home and more a well-oiled machine.

I was hooked.

Next, we visited Pittsburgh, home to another highly regarded mortuary school. If I chose Pittsburgh, I'd work with Striffler Funeral Homes—another NSM member with multiple locations across the city. The only problem? Pittsburghers don't cross rivers. It didn't matter if there was a bridge every few blocks—folks stayed on their side. It was funeral home loyalty with a built-in geographical boundary.

The real perk of Pittsburgh, though, was weekends in East Liverpool, Ohio, where one of Dad's closest friends ran Dawson Funeral Home. They lived on a tree farm in a beautifully restored barn, and down the road was a dairy that sold fresh milk in glass bottles, with the cream still floating on top. A lactose-intolerant person's nightmare, but for me? Heaven in a bottle.

After weighing my options, I ultimately chose Boston. I was engaged, ready to start a new chapter, and could already taste the clam chowder.

But fate had other plans.

My fiancée—half Polish and half German—had always wanted to visit Poland. This was 1980. Poland was still Communist, and travel wasn't exactly as easy as hopping on Expedia. But off she went. Three weeks in the days of no cell phones and expensive long-distance meant radio silence. Then, a few days before her scheduled return, the phone finally rang.

"I love you, but . . ."

Uh-oh.

Turns out, she had fallen in love with someone in Poland and decided to stay.

Well, that was a plot twist I didn't see coming.

Suddenly, Boston lost its charm. Lobster rolls, Fenway Park, even pahking the cah—they all felt flat.

To this day, I regret not going to Boston. It would have been an amazing experience, both personally and professionally. But looking back, I know it was probably the best thing that never happened to me. Instead, I followed Vic's path after all and enrolled at DIMS.

It was time to start over—again.

Part 3

COLLEGE, CAREERS, AND
CANINE COMPANIONS

INTERLUDE:
A FEW FINAL STORIES
BEFORE LEAVING MY
COLLEGE YEARS BEHIND

Texas Wesleyan College was a lot like Nolan—small classes, familiar faces, and best of all, new girls to meet.

I settled on a BBA in Management for one simple reason: it required no science classes. That's it. That was the logic. First semester? Fifteen hours on the books.

I didn't know many people at TWC, aside from Mike—who, funnily enough, was still holding a grudge over the infamous funeral home bathroom incident. (Honestly, I can't blame him.) But new school meant new friends, and I quickly made lifelong connections, some of whom still put up with me to this day.

Despite its tiny size, TWC had three fraternities: Lambda Chi Alpha, Sigma Phi Epsilon (Sig Ep), and Pi Kappa Alpha (Pikes). My brother Vic had been a Sig Ep, and I assumed I'd follow in his footsteps.

But there was a problem.

Sig Ep had been put on a two-year probation (clearly, they had a lot of fun the year before), so they had no new pledges. Because of that, their membership had dwindled down to about five guys in total—not exactly the thriving brotherhood I was looking for.

So, I pledged Lambda Chi, along with eight other guys. It turned out to be a great decision.

But before we go there, let's take a detour into one of my less-than-bright ideas.

When Vic was at TWC, his fraternity knew how to party. Unfortunately, I witnessed some of it firsthand. One time, when our parents were conveniently out of town, Vic and his fraternity brothers threw a banger. And since Vic couldn't kick me out, I stuck around, watching in awe as these guys drank anything and everything.

A few days later, Nolan had a half-day, and I rushed home, craving a Coke float—a simple mix of Coke and ice cream.

Problem: No Coke. No milk.

Solution: Replicate what Vic's frat brothers drank ice cream, vodka, and Kahlua.

Lesson learned: Just because fraternity guys drink it doesn't mean you should.

At the time, I thought it was a delicious success. Feeling great, I decided to take things up a notch and reenact scenes from Westerns, slamming back straight whiskey like a cowboy.

Spoiler alert: Bad idea.

Just when I thought I had the afternoon to recover, Vic called and asked if I wanted to caddy for him at Shady Oaks. In my overly confident, possibly very drunk manner, I said yes.

Bad decision #2 of the day.

What happened next?

First few holes: Clubs were coming out of the bag sideways, and I was weaving across the fairway like a drunk sailor.

Hole five: Elevated tee box, where I teetered near the edge while Vic was teeing off.

Next thing I knew? I rolled down the hill, popped up at the bottom, and waved back like nothing happened.

Round over equaled caddy career over.

To top it off? Vic got blamed for getting me drunk.

Lessons learned:

1. Never drink a full pitcher of vodka ice cream float.
2. Never imitate cowboys drinking whiskey.
3. Never caddy while drunk.

Not long after that stellar performance, I met Clayne Fraser, who, upon arriving at TWC, declared that he was now going by "CD." (Why? No idea. But CD it was.) Like me, he was a Fort Worth guy, a fellow Lambda Chi pledge, and someone who shared my appreciation for golf, road trips, and good times. CD was also an athletic trainer at a big gym, meaning he had girls lining up to talk to him.

Whenever Dad had a funeral trip to a country cemetery, CD would often tag along. We started doing weekend funeral home road trips together—and before we knew it, we had made hundreds of them.

Fair warning: CD will pop up a lot in future stories.

TWC's small classes meant you really got to know your professors; some of them even became lifelong friends. Others? Lifelong clients. (Occupational hazard in the funeral business.) One of my favorites was Dr. Donnelly.

Dr. Donnelly's tests were all essay-based, which I absolutely loved (sarcasm intended). On the first one, I hadn't studied a lick, so I BS'd my way through every single question. Grade? A. But with a note at the bottom:

"Mr. Thompson, it is obvious you have read nothing about this subject, but anyone with storytelling skills (he may have actually said bullshit) like yours will go a long way. Next time, study the material."

From that moment on, I took every class he taught.

By my senior year, I needed eighteen hours in the fall and eighteen in the spring to graduate. That fall semester, I loaded up on fifteen business class hours and one "easy" three-hour elective: *History Since 1960*—a discussion-based class with no tests or homework.

Perfect, right?

Wrong.

I attended every class, actively participated, and yet . . . I failed. Apparently, the professor was a die-hard hippie who didn't appreciate my argument that computers were more influential than hippies.

I complained to Dr. Donnelly, who then took me to TWC's president, Dr. Fleming. The result? The history class disappeared from my transcript, and Dr. Donnelly created a special class for me. The new class requirements consisted of subscribing to *The Wall Street Journal*, finding an article each week, and telling him a story about it, and receiving a Pass or a Fail.

I passed.

With that fixed, I loaded up my last semester and aced every single class. Getting those straight A's was my proudest year in school. Take that, high school aptitude tests!

Just before my junior year, my dad decided it was time for a little father-son bonding trip to Syracuse, NY. Our destination? The Marcellus Casket Company.

Marcellus wasn't just a manufacturer—they made the Rolls-Royce of hardwood caskets, available in eight luxurious woods. They were meticulous about everything; from the way they dried the wood to their hand-rubbed finishes to their perfectly tailored interiors.

But this trip wasn't just a factory tour. We were invited to the

President's Penthouse atop the Syracuse Club, their lake house on Lake Skaneateles, and their private island on Lake Superior (accessible only by boat). Let's just say, the Marcellus knew how to live.

Everything about the factory screamed craftsmanship and tradition. Every piece of sawdust from cutting and sanding? Collected and burned to heat the factory in the winter. Every worker? A veteran with twenty, thirty, forty, or even fifty years of experience. These guys weren't just making caskets; they were creating works of art.

Then came the ski challenge. Being from Texas, I said yes, of course. Into the icy water I went—August or not, it felt like glacial runoff. For an hour and a half, I refused to let go of the rope, waving off every "cut it" signal until the boat nearly ran out of gas.

Next morning? Mr. Marcellus invited me to join him for a "morning plunge." I declined. Politely.

That trip had one other complication—it clashed with fall registration at Wesleyan. So, I called Buddy Carter, the long-time registrar at TWC and a family friend, and told him I needed to pre-register for the fall semester before I left.

With his signature humor, Mr. Carter replied:

"Sure, Thompson, but I want cash—no checks."

A few days later, I called again to double-check.

"Cash, Thompson. I want cash."

That gave me an idea. I calculated the cost for eighteen credit hours plus fees. Total? $987. I went to the bank and withdrew exactly $987 in brand-new $1 bills, unbundled them, then tossed them into a big paper sack and shook it up really good.

The next day, I walked into Mr. Carter's office with my sack in hand. We sorted out my fall schedule, and he gleefully said, "That will be $987. And I hope you brought cash."

With a grin, I lifted the sack and poured a mountain of $1 bills onto his desk. He burst out laughing. Then, we stuffed the bills back into the sack and walked to the finance office.

The ladies at the counter? Not amused.

Working part-time at L.O. Hammons turned out to be more than just folding shirts and ringing up socks—it was my crash course in salesmanship.

I learned really quickly that Dad's friends made excellent leads. Their wives, bless them, were fountains of information—sizes, styles, colors they liked, even what they grumbled about in the closet. Armed with that intel, I'd load up my car with two or three suits, a couple of sport coats, and some slacks, then drive straight to their offices.

Voilà—instant pop-up showroom.

I'd lay everything out, size them up, and before long, I was walking out the door with orders for a couple of suits, a sport coat, and some slacks. After alterations, I'd make a return trip, this time with shirts and ties to match. Just for good measure, I'd throw in a few pairs of socks and even some underwear—free of charge. Naturally, while they were admiring the "bonus," I'd sell them a few extra shirts on delivery.

It worked like a charm.

The only problem? I worked on commission, and I thought I needed every new suit that came in. At one point, I owned over ten colors of ultra-suede sport coats—all custom-made. Even with my healthy discount, I was spending more money than I was making.

Still, it was a great job, one that almost made me want to become a ragman. Almost.

LESSONS LEARNED FROM THIS CHAPTER OF MY LIFE

+ Balancing funerals and fashion makes for an interesting résumé.

+ If someone asks for cash, make it rain (literally).

+ If you ever go skiing in upstate New York, make sure the water isn't straight out of a glacier.

+ Luxury casket makers live in absolute hardwood-covered paradise.

+ Wearing a suit every day does wonders for your dating life.

That trip to Marcellus Casket Company was unforgettable, and so was my time at L.O. Hammons. Who knew that one day I'd be helping families pick out the very same caskets I once marveled at in Syracuse? Life sure has a funny way of coming full circle.

11

HENRY THE SHEEPDOG:
MY FURRY, FOUR-LEGGED WINGMAN

Sometime during that same year, my fiancée surprised me with an Old English Sheepdog puppy. Enter Henry—a fluffy, lovable, four-legged tornado of pure joy.

Now, don't get me wrong—I liked my friends well enough, but Henry? I loved Henry.

At the time, I was still cruising around in my chocolate-brown Camaro LT, complete with the first T-tops in Fort Worth, plush beige velour seats, and a stereo that could make your ears ring for days.

As a puppy, Henry would perch on my lap during drives, his fluffy head sticking out the window, tongue lolling in the breeze, living his absolute best doggie life. During my night shifts, he'd snuggle up with me in my oh-so-spacious twin bed at the Ritz Quarters (aka the funeral home's nightman room). Cozy, to say the least.

As weeks turned into months, Henry transformed from an adorable fluff ball into a massive, lovable beast—one who still believed he was lap-dog size. After one too many drives with eighty pounds of sheepdog attempting to co-pilot from my lap, I conceded defeat. It was time for a bigger car. Enter the infamous Mercury Cougar—a vehicle with enough space for Henry to stretch out *and* enough legroom for me to drive.

Henry approved of the upgrade—as long as he still got his front-seat privileges.

But why stop just upgrading my car? I decided my best buddy deserved a home fit for the king he was. So, I went all out and built Henry his very own doghouse—except, let's be honest, it was more like a luxury suite. A full-size storage building from Sears, it had air conditioning, furniture, and was nestled comfortably in my parents' backyard. Henry was officially living better than most college students I knew.

And his most outstanding talent? Attracting attention.

Back in those days, our funeral home was in the hospital district, which came with a unique perk: an influx of young Irish nurses, freshly recruited to work at the hospitals. Most lived in the apartments behind the funeral home and were young, fun, and (let's be honest) very cute.

Henry and I had a routine of nightly and early-morning walks. And wouldn't you know it? The nurses LOVED Henry.

Floppy ears and big puppy eyes? Check.

Irresistible charm? Check.

Giant, lovable goofball energy? Double check.

Every time we walked by those apartments, Henry would practically get mobbed by nurses cooing over him. Since I had a fiancée, I kept things strictly at the harmless-flirting level. But Henry? He was shameless. He soaked up every bit of affection, happily wagging his tail like he owned the place.

Good boy, Henry. Good boy.

During this time, my only real struggle was the morning rush. Leo relieved me at 6:50 a.m., leaving me barely enough time to run home, shower, change clothes, and speed to TWC for my 8 a.m. class. And with Henry in the mix, I also had to feed and settle my furry co-pilot for the day.

This extra task consistently made me a tad late for class. And because I was always short on time, I developed a habit of parking in the no-parking zone—right by the building entrance.

And, like clockwork . . .

Parking ticket.

Parking ticket.

Parking ticket.

I was convinced the campus parking officers had memorized my schedule by heart.

So, was Henry the best dog ever? Absolutely.

Did he upgrade my social life? Without a doubt.

Was he worth every parking ticket in the world? One hundred percent.

Henry wasn't just a dog; he was my four-legged best friend, co-pilot, and the greatest wingman a guy could ask for. And while my college years were filled with classes, work, and a never-ending juggling act, they were made better (and much more entertaining) by one very special, very fluffy, very mischievous sheepdog named Henry.

12

PARKING TICKETS,
THE DEAN'S WRATH,
AND LIBRARY REVELATIONS

Fast forward to a week before graduation, when I received the kind of summons no soon-to-be graduate wants to hear: "The Dean needs to see you."

Now, when the Dean of Students calls you in just before graduation, it's never to ask if you'll miss the cafeteria food. And I knew this wasn't going to be a pat on the back for my contributions to campus life. Nope, something was up.

I arrived at Dr. Balcom's office, and after a few obligatory pleasantries about how much I "must have enjoyed" my time at Wesleyan, we finally got to the point. Dr. Balcom leaned back in his chair, steepling his fingers like a man about to deliver a serious moral lesson.

He started by sharing a cautionary tale about a mysterious car that had been parked in a no-parking zone for what he guessed was the past year, collecting a staggering number of unpaid parking tickets.

"We had quite the time trying to figure out who the owner was," he said with a slow smile, clearly enjoying himself. "No parking sticker, no registration in our system. The trail finally led to Holiday Lincoln Mercury, who eventually led us . . . to you."

And there it was. The jig was up.

With a dramatic flourish, he pulled out a thick stack of parking tickets, bound together with a rubber band, and dropped them on his desk. The sound was as heavy as my heart.

"Mr. Thompson," he said, tapping the pile. "Any idea how many parking violations this is?"

"A hundred?" I guessed, going for the high end.

"Close. Ninety-eight."

He leaned forward, resting his elbows on the desk. "So . . . how do you plan to take care of this before graduation?"

It was at this moment that I realized my financial standing was about to take a significant hit. The idea of bartering or negotiating flickered across my mind, but what was I going to offer? A future funeral discount?

We haggled like two men buying a used car, both wincing at the final number like we were splitting the bill at an overpriced steakhouse. In the end, we reached a compromise that was painful, but survivable.

With that financial disaster resolved, I figured I was home free—just a simple matter of waiting for graduation day.

Not so fast.

Before officially receiving my diploma, I had one final bureaucratic hurdle: I needed to get a clearance slip from the library confirming that I had no overdue books or outstanding fees.

Easy, right?

Except for one tiny problem.

I had never been to the library.

In four years.

For a brief moment, I considered just walking in blind and hoping I stumbled upon the right desk, but I decided to ask for directions instead. A kind soul pointed me toward the mysterious building I had avoided my entire college career.

When I walked in, I was hit with a wall of silence, broken only by the occasional clicking of typewriters and the shuffling of books. The librarian at the front desk—an older woman with glasses that looked like they could pierce my soul—peered at me with a mix of surprise and suspicion.

"Can I help you?" she asked, eyeing me as if she was certain I was lost.

"Yes," I said, confidently. "I need a note stating I don't owe anything."

She tilted her head. "And you are?"

"Martin Thompson."

She nodded and flipped through a massive logbook. After a moment, she raised an eyebrow. "You've been here four years, and this is your first time in the library?"

I cleared my throat. "That's correct."

She sighed, shook her head, and scribbled something on a slip of paper. "Here you go," she said, handing it to me like a doctor handing over a prescription for common sense.

And with that, I had completed the last of my pre-graduation obligations.

A week later, I walked across that stage, diploma in hand—parking tickets paid, library record cleared, and total time spent in the library officially clocking in at under five minutes.

My mom summed up the occasion in a way only she could. As she sat watching my fellow students receive their diplomas, she remarked, "Some graduated Magna Cum Laude, some Summa Cum Laude, and some just Cum Laude. But all I could think was: Laude, that boy graduated!"

LESSONS FROM MY GRADUATION WEEK

1. If you rack up 98 parking tickets, the Dean will eventually find you.

2. Never assume a funeral discount counts as currency.

3. The library is real, even if you've never set foot inside it.

4. Librarians have a sixth sense for detecting nonsense.

5. At graduation, honors don't matter as much as walking across the stage.

13

HARVESON & COLE: FROM RAILROAD MAN TO FUNERAL DIRECTOR

To understand the future of funeral service, sometimes you have to look back—way back. For me, that story begins with Harveson & Cole, the funeral home where it all started.

The year was 1911. Quincy Adams Harveson—a retired railroad man with a presidential name and a knack for reinvention—suddenly found himself in a new career. He'd been working at the Fort Worth train station, where he struck up a friendship with the owner of Sloane Undertaking Co. Then tragedy hit: a deadly disease swept through the city, and Harveson ended up burying nearly every member of Mr. Sloane's family. Heartbroken and worn down, Mr. Sloane finally handed Harveson the keys to the mortuary. Just like that, a railroad man became a funeral director.

By the 1920s, the days of holding funerals in living rooms were fading, and that two-room office wasn't cutting it anymore. Harveson upgraded by renting the basement, first, and second floors of the Masonic Lodge on Magnolia Street. Not only did this give him more space, it also tied him neatly into the railroad crowd and the Masons—two groups you definitely wanted on your side in those days.

Of course, funeral homes back then had to get creative just to stay afloat. Harveson and Cole ran a private switchboard, basically an early answering service. And since cell phones were still a century away, Harveson even came up with a flag-signaling system: if Dr. John Doe was urgently needed, someone in downtown Fort Worth would hang a specific flag out of a window, hoping the good doctor saw it and got the message. Was it high-tech? No. Was it effective? Sometimes. But hey, in 1920 that was practically Silicon Valley.

Somewhere along the line, Quincy's only daughter married Grover Cleveland Cole—because apparently presidential names were a family tradition. Cole jumped into the business, his sons followed, and suddenly Harveson & Cole was a full-on family affair.

Then came my dad, fresh off World War II. He joined Harveson & Cole and brought with him a large part of Fort Worth's Catholic community. Serving Catholic families out of a Masonic Lodge was, let's say, a delicate balancing act. It didn't take long before Dad decided we needed our own space. In 1957, he bought a stately old house on 8th Avenue—along with the neighboring homes around it—and turned the main residence into what quickly became Fort Worth's premier funeral home. That spot faithfully served generations until 2020, when I bought the business and moved us again, this time with an eye toward modern funeral service.

And the name? Believe it or not, we didn't add "Thompson's" to Harveson & Cole until 1980. My guess is Dad didn't want to rock the boat too soon, but eventually, our family name landed on the door. Better late than never.

So, from a two-room undertaking parlor to a Masonic Lodge with flag signals, to the big brick home on 8th Avenue, and finally to today's modern operation, Harveson & Cole's story is the story of funeral service itself: constantly changing, constantly adapting, but always rooted in care, family, and just enough ingenuity to get by.

14

MORTUARY MADNESS

L et's talk about a unique problem in the funeral profession: we might be the only industry still struggling to agree on what to call ourselves.

Once upon a time, we were undertakers. Then we became morticians. Then funeral directors. These days, depending on where you go, you'll hear everything from Funeral Service Providers to Funeral Arrangers to End-of-Life Specialists. Some places even call themselves *Family Life Centers*—which, let's be honest, sounds less like a funeral home and more like a picnic pavilion at the park.

At this rate, you need a glossary just to keep up with our job titles.

And sometimes, those shifting names can cause real problems.

Case in point: Years ago, I got summoned to federal jury duty —along with over a hundred other unlucky souls. The case? A drug lord and a murder trial. The judge announced this could drag on for nine months to a year. Not exactly a great forecast for a guy with a business to run, a family at home, and, most importantly, a golf game that required regular attention.

Then came the lifeline. The judge rattled off the list of exempt professions: members of the Armed Services, doctors, and—wait for it—morticians. All you had to do was show your credentials.

So, there I was, lined up with a bunch of doctors, feeling entirely out of place—like I'd crashed a medical conference wearing the wrong nametag. One by one, they flashed their medical licenses. When it was my turn, I proudly handed over my Funeral Director and Embalmer license.

The clerk frowned. "I'm sorry, sir, but you have to be a licensed *Mortician*."

I blinked. "That's what I am."

She shook her head. "No, sir. Your license says Funeral Director. Not Mortician."

I pointed at my credentials. "It's the same thing!"

She crossed her arms, unimpressed. "No, sir. The exemption is for Morticians. You're a Funeral Director."

I asked if I could speak with the judge. She gave me a look that could curdle milk and sent me to stand off to the side like I was in detention.

Finally, the judge returned. The clerk, clearly irritated, handed him my license. He glanced at it, then at me, and broke into a smile.

"He's exempt."

Just like that, I was free to go. Golf game saved.

So maybe we can't agree on what to call ourselves—but when it comes to federal jury duty, I'll answer to *anything* that gets me out of a year-long drug lord trial.

15

THE EVOLUTION OF FUNERAL HOMES AND LIMOS

leet color used to be a BIG DEAL in the funeral profession. Back in the day, every funeral home had its own distinct color—so when a funeral procession rolled through, you knew exactly which funeral home was handling it just by the color of the cars.

Harveson & Cole? Briar Rose.

And let me tell you—Briar Rose was a choice.

Our fleet consisted of two Cadillac Brougham sedans, two Cadillac hearses (or "funeral coaches" as we say today), three Cadillac limousines, two station wagons (one for making calls, the other was my mom's—because nothing says "mom car" like a station wagon), a white panel van, and some poor junker used for errands, often from someone who traded it in to pay for a funeral.

By my junior year at Texas Wesleyan, I bought one of the limos for my side business—a limousine service. To upgrade it, I removed the jump seats and replaced them with a custom bar, ice bucket, and a TV with a VHS player I painted navy blue. When things were slow, I'd park in front of Billy Bob's on the Northside and give rides for $5 a person, taking people on a 15-minute loop through downtown Fort Worth. I made about $100 a night, which wasn't bad for a college kid.

Eventually, I convinced my dad to let me ditch Briar Rose and go with dark blue. Harveson & Cole went from looking like a giant floral arrangement on wheels to something sleek and sophisticated—one concertgoer, bar hopper, and $5 ride at a time.

16

THERE I GO AGAIN:
BACK TO THE BIG BOARD

n 1980, funeral service hadn't changed in decades. If you made it onto the big board, you were handling a case. If you weren't, well, maybe next time.

Now, "the Big Board" wasn't some abstract concept. It was literally a giant chalkboard in the break room that ran our lives. Every morning, Dad would stroll in and write out the day's funerals. At the top, he'd chalk the name of the deceased, the time of service, the place of service, and the cemetery.

Then came the assignments. Everyone in the building knew the code:

+ LD = Lead Car (usually Dad or my brother Vic—rank had its privileges).

+ PB = Pallbearer Car (a funeral director).

+ CC = Casket Coach, a.k.a. the hearse (also handled by a funeral director).

+ Fam = Family Cars, typically two, driven by junior funeral directors who hadn't annoyed Dad that week.

+ Flow = Flower Car—the absolute bottom rung of the ladder. No glamour, no dignity, just you and a van stuffed with floral sprays wilting in the Texas heat.

The first time my name showed up on that board, I thought I'd made the big leagues. Didn't matter that I was on "Flow." I was officially in the game. Over time, I clawed my way up the ranks: Flow → Family → Pallbearer Car → Casket Coach. It was like a funeral home version of minor league baseball, only with more polyester suits and less bubble gum. And if you ever made it to **LD?** That was our version of the Hall of Fame.

At our firm, we handled about 500 calls per year, and of those, maybe two families chose cremation. The rest were full-on traditional funerals, with more flowers than a beauty pageant on steroids. And oh, the sprays—the ultimate last-minute floral panic purchase. These were 10-inch foam squares packed with flowers that were about 24 hours away from giving up on life themselves. Florists charged $10 to $20, which was proof that the funeral industry wasn't the only business with a "creative" approach to pricing.

Dad was a floral perfectionist. If an arrangement was even slightly off-center, it was a personal insult to the art of symmetry. One of his favorite critiques was: *"Did Helen Keller place these arrangements?"* But if you tried to avoid the job altogether, you'd hear: *"Do I have to be the only one working around here?"*

So, the process went like this:

1. Receive flowers at the funeral home and haul them to the stateroom.
2. Rearrange them according to Dad's strict, unspoken floral commandments.
3. Load them into the Flower Car and deliver them to the church.
4. Haul them to the cemetery.
5. And finally, deliver them to the family home.

And all of this was done in Texas summers while wearing suits—which, if you've never tried it, is like walking through a sauna wrapped in wool. The two weeks of winter weren't much better, just the opposite kind of misery.

Still, I didn't complain. I was on the board, and that meant I was part of the show.

But the industry itself was beginning to shift. By the early 1980s, society was on the move. People were leaving their hometowns for work, marriage, and adventure, which meant not everyone was being buried in the family plot anymore. And then, something shocking started happening: more families began saying, "Mom wants to be cremated."

Now, Dad was *not* a fan of cremation. His standard response? *"I've seen many things come and go."* Which, to be fair, is exactly what every industry veteran says right before the future runs them over.

Back then, we didn't offer much for cremation families. The process was cold, transactional, and minimal—fill out some paperwork, sign a form, and that was it. No service, no ceremony, nothing.

Looking back, that was a major failure on our part. It took years for our industry to realize that just because a family chose cremation didn't mean they didn't want to celebrate their loved one.

The turning point came when families started coming back and saying, *"We still want cremation . . . but can we also have a service?"*

And suddenly, it was as if a light bulb went off. Who knew people still wanted to gather, tell stories, and remember their loved ones—even if they opted out of burial?

That shift changed everything.

But not before the funeral industry dragged its feet for way too long.

74

17

THE DISCO
COWBOY CHRONICLES

We're going to switch gears to the lighter side of 1980—because while funeral service was slowly evolving, my wardrobe was changing faster than a Saturday night playlist.

Nineteen eighty was absolute chaos for me: two full-time jobs at Thompson's Harveson & Cole, running my own limousine business, getting left at the altar (you know the story), and—oh yes—Urban Cowboy fever hit Fort Worth like a rhinestone hurricane.

At the start of the decade, I was still fully committed to disco life: wide collars, gold chains, and enough polyester to qualify as a workplace fire hazard.

Then *Urban Cowboy* happened.

Overnight, the dance floors shifted. Discos closed, country bars opened, and suddenly everyone was two-stepping instead of doing the Hustle. Even L.O. Hammons, where I worked, went all in—rolling out a Western clothing line that looked like it had been swiped from a George Strait wardrobe truck: designer jeans, pearl-snap shirts, exotic skin boots.

So, naturally, I thought: *Why not?*

I jumped in with both feet—literally, into a pair of stovepipe eel-skin boots that squeaked when I walked.

One night, feeling confident in my new cowboy persona, I strutted into Cowtown Country in full Urban Cowboy regalia. That's when I ran into a girl from high school, a girl I barely spoke to back then. Only now, she was still dressed for Studio 54 in a white jumpsuit straight out of *Saturday Night Fever*.

Trying to be smooth, I opened with my best cowboy-meets-disco line:

"Is that some kind of disco outfit you have on?"

(Somehow, she didn't walk away.)

In fact, that corny one-liner led to an entire relationship . . . and eventually, marriage. Go figure—a guy in squeaky eel-skin boots and a girl in a disco jumpsuit.

But I digress.

What did I learn in 1980?

1. Funeral service was changing, even if we hadn't seen it yet.

2. Cremation was here to stay, whether my dad liked it or not.

3. If you're going to wear cowboy boots, you'd better commit.

4. And most importantly: Never underestimate the power of a bad pickup line.

18

BIG BUCKS AND
BROWN MGB

ooking back, 1980 was a pivotal year. I was making what seemed, at the time, like serious money—and, of course, spending it just as fast.

+ **Day job at Thompson's Harveson & Cole (THC):** $8 an hour, at least 40 hours a week.

+ **Night gig at THC:** $12 an hour (time and a half), another 40 hours a week—though let's be honest, half of that was spent "sleeping on duty," one ear tuned to the phone, ready to grab it by the third ring.

+ **Side hustle at L.O. Hammons:** helped keep my clothing addiction from reaching "financial intervention" levels.

+ **Limousine business:** pure walking-around cash—for dates, bar tabs, and impulse purchases that only seemed smart in the moment.

When I did the math, I realized I was pulling in over $1,000 a week. To twenty-two-year-old me, that meant one thing: I had officially *made it.*

Naturally, I did what any responsible young man would do with his newfound fortune: I bought a new car.

And not just any car—a chocolate-brown MGB.

Now, this sleek little two-seater British sportscar was not exactly designed for a skinny Texas-guy like me. But that wasn't the real issue. The issue was Henry, my Old English Sheepdog, who still firmly believed his rightful place in any moving vehicle was planted directly on my lap.

After some near-death driving experiences, I finally convinced him the passenger seat was his kingdom. He accepted—reluctantly—but once he settled in, he looked like royalty. With his long hair blowing in the wind, he resembled a cross between shag carpet and Winston Churchill.

My favorite part? Watching guys roll up on the passenger side, expecting to see a beautiful woman riding shotgun—only to lock eyes with eighty pounds of drooling sheepdog staring them down. Henry always got the last laugh.

Even though I was "raking in the big bucks," I had a natural gift for spending it just as fast. In hindsight, I probably could have had a successful second career as a government budget consultant.

But then 1981 rolled around, and reality hit me with a three-point checklist:

+ I was getting married in the fall.
+ I was starting Mortuary Science School the day after my honeymoon.
+ Both school and marriage were going to cut deep into my work hours (and my bar tab).

Things were about to get very real.

19

I DO, CANCUN, AND THE
CASE OF THE MISSING SWIMSUITS

After our "I do's," our honeymoon in Cancun was full of surprises, proving that even the best-laid plans can lead to hilariously unexpected adventures.

In 1981, Cancun was still the new kid on the travel block. There were only a handful of hotels, and the Camino Real was the crown jewel—a stunning resort that, unfortunately, was a bit out of my budget thanks to previous financial decisions involving cars and clothes.

So, we settled for the brand-new Marriott, which was halfway up the island and still in the process of being spruced up for an upcoming visit from the President of the United States, including hand-sanding the beach—which, honestly, was as ridiculous as it sounds.

There weren't many restaurants yet, but there was a jet ski rental (on the bay side), a mosquito conservatory (not officially, but the jet ski rental was in the middle of it), and a somewhat reliable bus service to shuttle tourists between these exotic attractions.

Now, it may surprise you to know I have a habit of striking up conversations with strangers. Early in our trip, we met an older couple—which, considering I was twenty-three, meant they were probably in their mid-forties. The wife was a travel agent scouting

Cancun, and the husband was just along for the ride, mostly hanging out alone at the pool.

One afternoon, my wife and I took a long walk down the beach. Between the Marriott and Playa Blanca was a long stretch of virgin beach, almost deserted—until we stumbled upon a large group of people who had seemingly lost their bathing suits.

Yep. A full-blown nudist beach.

We nervously laughed, turned around, and hightailed it back to the Marriott.

And that's when I saw him. The lonely guy from the pool, walking straight toward the nudists. I stopped him and said, "You're not going to believe this, but there are a bunch of skinny dippers up ahead."

His response? "Really?"

Merrily, he continued his way. I guess he was about to lose his bathing suit, too.

We arrived home from our honeymoon on a Sunday night in early September, and reality hit me like a brick wall: the next morning at 7:00 a.m., I was starting mortuary school. Not only that, but I'd also had to say goodbye to my job at L.O. Hammons, my full-time nightman job was now weekends only, and Dad had given me a raise so I could afford DIMS. Oh, and did I mention I was now an instant dad to a six-year-old?

Candice, Eleanor's daughter, was suddenly my daughter too. She was a bright, curious kid who was taking this whole "new family" thing in stride—though not without her share of funny moments. Poor Candice even got the Henry treatment. Just like Eleanor, she stepped outside one day only to be body-checked by my overexcited dog, who thought everyone was fair game for his full-speed NFL tackles. It was like Henry was the official hazing committee for our new family members.

Candice and I exchanged our share of bonding stories, too. I'll never forget going to our first parent-teacher conference together. Eleanor and I walked in ready to hear about grades and behavior, but we spent the first ten minutes convincing the teachers I was really Candice's dad and not her much older brother. At 140 pounds soaking wet and barely looking my age of twenty-three, I didn't exactly scream "father figure." But eventually, they believed me—and we all laughed.

Back at home, Henry's antics continued. We had a game where he'd take off at full speed, circle about twenty yards out, and barrel toward me like a heat-seeking missile. Then I'd catch his front legs, spin him to the side, and he'd land gracefully. We repeated this until I ... or rather *he* ... got tired.

I forgot to mention Henry's game to Eleanor and Candice, which meant they were blindsided every time they stepped into the backyard—until *they* got tired of it.

20

DINGY SCHOOL DAYS, MIDNIGHT CALLS, AND THE DOCTOR WITH THE POLAROID

Mortuary school was five days a week, 7:30 a.m. to 12:30 p.m., in a building that looked like it hadn't been updated since the Great Depression. The student center alone was a time capsule of neglect torn-up vinyl chairs that had been through wars—possibly literal ones; a pool table missing half the felt, making every shot a gamble; and a ping-pong table with a massive crack down the middle, ensuring every game ended in an argument.

The school had no cafeteria or breakroom, so twice a day, the Roach Coach (our affectionate term for the food truck) would pull up. The menu? A mystery. I made the mistake of ordering a chicken sandwich once, only to discover that it was neither chicken nor much of a sandwich.

It was clear that surviving mortuary school would require more than just knowledge, it would require a strong stomach.

After class, I'd drive back to Fort Worth and put in hours at THC. Then came the real fun—my new on-call duty. Every third night, the new nightman would call me at 2 a.m. to make a removal, embalm, and return home just in time to shower and drive forty-plus miles back to Dallas for class.

It was a perfectly miserable schedule, and I was running on caffeine, adrenaline, and the stubborn determination to finish school. I was also learning the trade the old-school way—hands-on, at ungodly hours, with little sleep and plenty of embalming fluid.

Meanwhile, Eleanor was keeping the home front steady, and Candice was getting used to the idea of having a dad who was always either gone or dead tired. She didn't mind bragging at school, though: "My daddy works at the funeral home." That line got her plenty of wide-eyed stares from classmates, and more than a few raised eyebrows from teachers.

Speaking of ungodly hours, let's talk about the night I got pulled over in my limo.

At this point, I was still occasionally taking limo gigs when I could fit them between school and work. One night, I got booked to drive a doctor and his much-younger girlfriend from Fort Worth to Dallas.

The itinerary was, shall we say, ambitious: first stop: Fortnight at Neiman's (fancy shopping for fancy people); second stop: The French Room at The Adolphus Hotel (a place where even the butter looked expensive); then back home to Fort Worth.

While the couple shopped, the doctor asked me to buy a Polaroid camera and extra film. I found the camera, returned to Neiman's, and waited in my navy-blue Cadillac limousine. Then came the problem.

The French Room was on a one-way street, directly behind me, meaning I had to:

1. Turn left at the next street.
2. Turn left again to get to Main Street.
3. Turn left once more onto Elm.

What I didn't know? Dallas had just put up brand-new "No Turn" signs. I figured, "No Turn" can't mean no left on red if it's a one-way to a one-way . . . right?"

Wrong. I signaled left, made my turn, and—red and blue lights flashed in my mirror.

Officer: "Do you know why I pulled you over?"

Me: "Uh . . . because I made a legal turn?"

Officer: "Nope. New law. No turns. Period."

I was getting two tickets, and as I tried to process my bad luck, I noticed the doctor getting out of the limo—with his brand-new Polaroid in hand, which he promptly used to start snapping pictures. I was too tired to question it.

Dallas had a Night Court, and the officer explained my hearing would be scheduled for the following week. Sure enough, seven days later I had to show up in the middle of the night to argue my case. The judge took one look at the situation, sighed, and said, "I'll reduce it to one ticket. Just don't turn left anymore."

Great.

So, after losing sleep and paying a fine that was more than I made on that limo ride, I had learned another expensive lesson.

And if that entire night wasn't bizarre enough, I saw the doctor a week later. He handed me an envelope. Inside? A set of Polaroids.

Me, standing next to the cop.

A close-up of the ticket.

The cop writing me up.

His girlfriend laughing in the backseat.

"If you ever want to remember your first Night Court experience," he said with a grin.

Back at home, I showed Eleanor the photos. She rolled her eyes, and Candice got a kick out of the one where the cop looked like he was scolding me. At least somebody thought it was funny.

LESSONS FROM MY FIRST YEAR OF MORTUARY SCHOOL

1. Sleep is for the weak.

2. The Roach Coach is a gamble—eat at your own risk.

3. If your limo client asks for a Polaroid camera, don't ask questions.

4. Dallas cops take No Turn signs VERY seriously.

5. Never assume a ticket is the worst part of your night. Sometimes, it's the Polaroids.

THE FUNERAL PROFESSION:
OLDER THAN THE OLDEST PROFESSION (WITH MORE DIGNITY)

— PART ONE —

L et's set the record straight—while another profession often claims the title of "the oldest," funeral service might just have them beat (and with a lot more dignity). After all, people have been dying since the beginning of time, and somebody had to figure out what to do with them.

My journey into this ancient and honorable calling didn't exactly begin with academic excellence. After college, I went to work full-time at Thompson's Harveson & Cole Funeral Home under my dad's watchful eye. That's where the real learning started.

One day, Dad told me I had to give a speech to the Serra Club —a room full of well-respected Catholic men, many of them Fort Worth's movers and shakers. I was in my early twenties, had zero public-speaking experience, and was supposed to educate them about a subject most people avoid at all costs. I was terrified.

So, I did what any nervous young funeral director would do— I prepared for the worst. I wrote my speech, practiced in the mirror, and braced myself for humiliation. Then I had an idea: if I was going to talk about funerals, why not start with a bit of humor?

I opened with:

"Thank you for inviting me to speak today. I want to start by giving you a brief history of funeral service. We like to think of ourselves as the oldest profession, even though I know another one has that claim to fame. I'd just like to think we're held in slightly higher regard."

Then I dramatically flipped open a Bible and said:

"The first recorded funeral service? Right here in Genesis, Chapter 4: Cain and Abel. After Cain took care of Abel, their parents, Adam and Eve, called Guy Thompson to handle the arrangements. It's right here in the Bible my dad gave me."

Sometimes, that got a laugh. Other times—blank stares. I eventually retired that joke for my own sanity.

From there, I launched my version of funeral history:

+ **Ancient Egyptians**: Embalmers carefully removed organs, placed them in canopic jars, dried the body with natron salts and sunlight, and wrapped it in linen soaked with resin. Their goal wasn't just preservation—it was preparing the body for a spiritual journey along the "Starry Path," where one day the deceased would be reunited with their organs and live again. (So far, no one's shown up asking for their jars back, but I keep checking.)

+ **Roman period**: The Romans turned funerals into theater. Families hired "wailers" to mourn loudly in public; the more noise, the more important one appeared. Houses overflowed with flowers—partly to display wealth but mostly to mask the smell of decomposition, since embalming wasn't yet available. Processions wound through the streets with musicians, torches, and banners announcing the life of the deceased. It was grief mixed with show business.

+ **Civil War America**: This is where Dr. Thomas Holmes enters the picture. Soldiers were dying far from home, and grieving families wanted their boys brought back. Holmes, a surgeon, invented an arterial embalming technique that allowed bodies to be preserved long enough for transport. For the first time in American history, the dead could "come home." Without Holmes, thousands of families would never have seen their sons again.

That whirlwind history always amazed people. But back then, I was just parroting facts. Only later did I realize I was telling the story of how funeral service adapted again and again to what families needed most.

Closing Button: *And that's how my very first speech convinced me of one thing—if history didn't keep people awake, at least my jokes might.*

THE FUNERAL PROFESSION:
OLDER THAN THE
OLDEST PROFESSION
(WITH MORE DIGNITY)

— PART TWO —

After Dad's Cain-and-Abel bit bombed more times than I care to admit, I pivoted. Instead of biblical funeral history, I opened with a joke. It wasn't always funeral-related, but it bought me time and loosened the room.

One of my go-tos was this whole story about a talking dog:

A man drives past a house with a sign that says, "Talking Dog—$20." He pulls over, thinking no way, and goes to the door. The owner answers, and he says, "I'm here about your talking dog for $20."

Come in he says.

Fred he calls, and in trots a Golden Retriever. The man says, "Go ahead, do your thing."

The dog says, "Hi, I'm Fred, I'm a talking dog."

The man says, "What's your story?"

Fred says, "When I was a pup, I was owned by a guy who was a bad guy. He learned early on what I could do. So, he would put me in a room and have me listen to his friends. I could tell him who was stealing his money, who might be about to put a hit on him, and other things like that. It wasn't too bad; he gave me good dog treats, and I had a good dog bed. One day, this beautiful Golden Doodle named Matilda walked in, and we fell in love. We got married, and she started having puppies. Matilda started getting worried about my job and the guy and wanted me to find another job. I initially started working for the police department, then transitioned to the FBI, and eventually joined the CIA. We solved many crimes, and I even prevented a major terrorist attack one day. Matilda started getting worried that this job was getting dangerous, and again, she wanted me to find a safer job, so I became a dog trainer. And since I can speak both dog and human, I can train a dog faster and better than a human. That's my story."

The man is stunned and speaks. "Why in the world are you selling this dog for only $20?"

The owner shrugs. "Because he's a liar—he made all that up."

That joke usually landed much better than the Cain and Abel story. Once the crowd laughed, I'd follow with:

"Well, I don't have Fred the Talking Dog here today, so you're stuck with this talking funeral director. And since 'funeral' begins with 'fun,' let's take a fun look at funeral service."

At that point in my career, I thought I had a good understanding of history. I told the audience that funerals date back 3,500 years to the Ancient Egyptians. Turns out I was off by about 3,000 years.

The real pioneers were the Chinchorro people of Chile and Peru, who were embalming their dead over 7,000 years ago—long before the first pyramid was ever sketched on papyrus. What made the Chinchorro remarkable was their inclusiveness: they preserved the remains of everyone, not just kings or nobles. Elders, children, infants, and even miscarried babies were cared for with the same dignity. Their methods were astonishing: they removed organs and replaced them with plant fibers or animal hair; they sometimes stabilized and reshaped the body using natural clays and textiles to restore a recognizable form; and they developed three distinct techniques—the Black Mummy, Red Mummy, and Mud Coat. In short, the world's first funeral directors weren't Egyptian—they were South American. And I'd been giving funeral speeches for years without even mentioning them.

As if that gap weren't enough, I also left out Colonial America's rum-soaked funerals.

In the 1600s and 1700s, funerals were more about social gatherings than solemn reflection. Families hosted all-night wakes at home. Food flowed, but liquor flowed faster. The rum bill was often the most significant expense of the entire funeral. Guests left with gifts—black gloves, scarves, or even gold rings. At Waitstill Winthrop's funeral (grandson of the Massachusetts governor), mourners received over sixty gold rings. His funeral cost nearly one-fifth of his estate.

It got so out of hand that in 1761, Massachusetts passed the "Act to Retrench the Extraordinary Expense at Funerals," which outlawed excessive alcohol and gift-giving. Anyone caught handing out rum at a wake faced a fifty-pound fine—a fortune then.

So, while the Egyptians were perfecting embalming, the Chinchorro were proving everyone deserved preservation, and Colonial Americans were perfecting the open bar. My early speeches hit the highlights, but it took me decades to realize just how colorful and wide-ranging funeral history really was.

Closing Button: *Turns out, the only thing older than funeral service is people arguing over who's buying the next round.*

THE FUNERAL PROFESSION:
OLDER THAN THE
OLDEST PROFESSION
(WITH MORE DIGNITY)

— PART THREE —

Before the 1800s, funerals were strictly a family affair. Relatives and neighbors washed and prepared the body, dug the grave, and held wakes at home.

But as cities swelled, church graveyards overflowed, and decomposition outpaced comfort levels. That's when furniture makers and carriage builders saw opportunity: sell coffins, provide hearses, and eventually offer full-service funerals. These tradesmen became known as *Undertakers*—not because they wrestled The Rock, but because they "undertook" the responsibility of handling death.

The Civil War changed everything. With soldiers dying far from home, Dr. Thomas Holmes introduced embalming so families could see their loved ones again. When Abraham Lincoln was assassinated, his body toured the country by train, stopping in several cities for public viewings. At each city, an embalmer provided careful touch-ups to maintain his appearance for mourners. That experience helped convince Americans that embalming was here to stay.

By the late 1800s, embalming was standard, and undertakers expanded their role. The term itself, though, felt a little grim, so the profession rebranded: first to *Morticians* (fancy, but a bit too "magician of the dead"), and later to *Funeral Directors*—a title that reflected not just burial, but guiding families through loss.

By the time I entered the business in the 1970s, the transformation was complete. Traditional funerals were the norm, cremation barely existed, and embalming in the kitchen had mercifully faded away.

Closing Button: *We may have changed titles—from Undertaker to Funeral Director—but the job description has always been the same: don't mess it up.*

THE FUNERAL PROFESSION:
OLDER THAN THE
OLDEST PROFESSION
(WITH MORE DIGNITY)

— PART FOUR —

F uneral service cruised along until the 1960s, when Jessica Mitford came along with her sharp pen. In 1963, she published *The American Way of Death*, an exposé accusing funeral directors of price-gouging widows and upselling grieving families.

Her book hit the industry like a thunderclap. Suddenly, families who never asked questions were scrutinizing price lists and wondering why a steel casket cost more than their first car. My father, along with directors across the country, found himself fielding tougher questions than ever.

Was everything she wrote wrong? Not entirely. And in 1984, the FTC stepped in with the Funeral Rule: itemized price lists, no forced bundles, and freedom to buy only what families wanted. Most funeral directors were already doing right by their communities, but the rule kept the few bad apples from giving us all a black eye.

Just as the dust settled, another tidal wave hit, cremation. In the 1960s, it was rare, but by the 1990s, it was everywhere. Cost, mobility, religious changes, and environmental concerns pushed it forward. By 2015, cremation had overtaken burial in the US, and the traditional funeral was no longer the default option.

In my forty years, I've seen funerals evolve from open-casket visitations to slideshow celebrations of life, from handwritten obituaries to online memorials, and from family plots to scattering ashes on mountaintops. Throughout it all, the profession continued to adapt. And so did my speech.

Closing Button: *Jessica Mitford may have changed how we did business, but she also guaranteed that families would never again buy a casket the way they bought a used car.*

THE FUNERAL PROFESSION:
OLDER THAN THE
OLDEST PROFESSION
(WITH MORE DIGNITY)

— PART FIVE —

I f you think embalming in the kitchen or rum-soaked wakes were strange, wait until you see what's next.

Green burials are on the rise: no embalming, biodegradable caskets, no vaults. Think of it as farm-to-table—but earth-to-earth. Some families choose tree pod burials, where your final act is helping grow an oak or willow.

Aquamation—"the spa treatment for the dearly departed"—is also gaining traction. Instead of fire, it uses water and alkali to accelerate what nature does over time. *Aquamation is a gentle, water-and-alkali process that accelerates what nature does over time, with a smaller carbon footprint than flame cremation.*

And technology keeps rewriting expectations:

+ **Livestreamed funerals** let Uncle Bob in Florida attend without leaving his recliner.

+ **AI-generated obituaries** are emerging (though if AI wrote mine, it would probably say, "He wore a coat and tie for services but preferred casual the rest of the time").

+ **Holograms** are now possible—imagine Grandpa projected at his own service, saying, "Surprise! I get the last word."

✤ **Digital memorials** are replacing static headstones. QR codes at gravesites can link to videos, photos, even interactive family trees.

But that's not all:

✤ **Biotech memorials,** where ashes or DNA are used to create gemstones, tattoos, or even living memorial plants.

✤ **Virtual reality remembrance,** where families "visit" a loved one's life in immersive 3D recreations.

✤ **Space memorials,** where a symbolic portion of ashes is launched into orbit or beyond—"ashes to stardust."

✤ **Eco-innovations,** like mushroom suits that turn remains into nutrient-rich soil without chemicals, or artificial reefs built from cremated remains to help restore ocean habitats.

Through it all, one thing hasn't changed: families still need compassion, guidance, and a steady hand. The customs may evolve, but the calling remains the same.

And so does my speech—only now, I tell it with fifty years of stories, mistakes, and maybe just a little more dignity.

Closing Button: *The future may bring holograms, QR codes, and even mushroom suits—but compassion never goes out of style.*

Part 4

A NEW CHAPTER:

BALANCING LIFE,
BUSINESS, AND LOSS

21

OUT OF SCHOOL,
GOLF GANGS,
AND THE LEGEND OF DIGGER

G raduating from mortuary school was supposed to be my grand entrance into full-time funeral service, but as it turned out, it was also my gateway into a whole new world of golf, gambling, and nicknames that stuck harder than embalming fluid on a bad day.

When I walked off campus for the last time, I heard the heavenly choir. This was it. No more tests, no more lectures, no more half-baked excuses for why I hadn't done an assignment.

Well, almost.

Before I could officially call myself a funeral director and embalmer, I had to head to Austin to take the state licensing exam. This was the big one, covering both—as the title implies—funeral directing and embalming.

By this point, I had eighteen years of education under my belt and had finally figured out how to study. Result? I aced both tests and was now an official apprentice in my field.

The apprenticeship lasted two years, requiring me to log one hundred cases for both funeral directing and embalming. But for the first time in my life, school was behind me. And with my new raise, I had enough money to do something I had always wanted: join a country club.

If you lived in Fort Worth and were serious about golf, you had a few elite choices:

+ Shady Oaks – Where Ben Hogan had walked the fairways and my brother was a member

+ Colonial – Home of the Colonial National Invitational golf tournament

+ Ridglea – Two great golf courses

+ River Crest – The blue-bloods club, where if you weren't born into the right family, good luck getting in

Then there was Woodhaven: a working man's club.

Even though I was making what I thought was good money, it wasn't Shady Oaks, Colonial, or River Crest money. So, I went with Woodhaven. Best decision I ever made.

Work and school had kept me away from golf for years, but that was about to change.

Woodhaven had a standing game every weekday except Monday, plus Saturday mornings and Sunday afternoons. They called it the gangsome, which was a rowdy, competitive, but welcoming group of guys who took their golf seriously but never themselves. Most of them were in their forties, fifties, and sixties, with the youngest guy in his midthirties. I was a mere twenty-four, but I was welcomed just the same.

The golf games were fun, with friendly betting that could get serious if you wanted it to. This is where I met Eddie Robinson.

If you grew up watching baseball, you knew who Eddie Robinson was. He had been a Major League player in the 1940s and '50s, then later became the general manager of the Texas

Rangers. Even in retirement, he was still involved as a scout. Several former Rangers players were also members of Woodhaven and the gangsome, so every game felt like I was playing with legends.

One day, as they were calling out the teams, someone yelled: "I've got Digger!"

Digger? Who the hell is that?

Turns out, the name came from Digger O'Dell, a character from the old radio and TV show *The Life of Riley*. Digger was the friendly undertaker, famous for lines like:

"It is I, Digby O'Dell, the friendly undertaker," and "I was just taking a stroll around the pond. I enjoy listening to the frogs croak."

At first, I wasn't sure about the nickname. But when you're the only funeral director in a golf group full of retired baseball players, you take what you can get. So, I embraced it. And just like that, "Digger" stuck.

Woodhaven wasn't just about golf, however; it was about lessons in life. They taught me how to play Gin. They ran a casino game once a week. And they taught me exactly how to get in trouble with my wife when I stayed out a little too late. For example, I learned that if you were supposed to be home by 6 p.m. and rolled in at 8:30 p.m., you better have one hell of an excuse or a good bottle of wine.

But the best part? The friendships.

Eddie Robinson became more than just a playing partner—he became a lifelong friend.

The truth is, Woodhaven was more about belonging to a group of guys who had been through life, had stories to tell, and were willing to take a young guy under their wing than it was about golf. It was about laughter, competition, and learning that life—like golf—isn't always fair, but you play the ball where it lies. And it was about earning a nickname that would follow me for the rest of my life.

22

THE OPTIMIST CLUB:
WHERE A GOOD MEAL
WENT TO DIE

When you're twenty-three and fresh out of mortuary school, you're not exactly roaming the streets looking for civic clubs to join. You go where you're invited, where they serve a decent lunch, and where the older guys might just toss a little business your way.

That's how I ended up at the Fort Worth Optimist Club. They met every Friday at noon at First United Methodist downtown. The church ladies knew how to cook—roast beef, mashed potatoes, banana pudding—the kind of meal that makes you glad you showed up. Well... most weeks, anyway.

The Optimist Club wasn't just about food. Their motto, *Friend of Youth*, was the real deal. They ran after-school programs, junior golf tournaments, and even a Little League on the Southside for underprivileged kids. The boys got new hats and shirts, team photos, and—best of all—a free snack after every game. It was a phenomenal program, and I was glad to be part of it.

But running all that took money. And money meant fundraisers:

1. **Christmas Tree Sales** – one lot on Lancaster & University, and one indoors at Will Rogers Coliseum where we sold "flocked" trees that looked like they'd survived a blizzard in Aspen. If you saw a snow-covered tree in a bank lobby back then, chances are we sold it.

2. **The Annual Charity Golf Tournament** – basically an excuse for businessmen to drink beer, call it "charity," and hack their way around the course.

I was all in—new member, new energy, new friendships. Which is how I ended up in a position I should've politely declined: *Program Chair.*

The title sounds important. It isn't. It just means you're responsible for booking the speaker every single Friday—except Christmas, Easter, and New Year's. Easy enough, right? Wrong. After I burned through the obvious choices (pastors, bankers, car dealers), I found myself scrambling. And that's when I made a decision that still haunts me.

I invited the brand-new Tarrant County Medical Examiner, Dr. Nizam Peerwani, to give a talk. Nice man. Very professional. Asked for a projector and screen, which should have been my first red flag.

Friday at 12:30, the food was terrific—the roast beef tender, the mashed potatoes creamy, the tea perfectly sweet. Then Dr. Peerwani took the podium. His subject: *The Role of the Medical Examiner in Forensic Science.*

Educational, I thought. Interesting, maybe.

Then came the slides.

Slide 1: A decomposed body in a shallow grave.

Slide 2: A point-blank gunshot wound.

Slide 3: A bloated corpse pulled from the Trinity River.

Slide 4: A particularly "memorable" suicide.

That's when the first man stood up and walked out. Then another. And another. By Slide 6, half the room was gone. By Slide 10, the survivors fell into three categories:

1. People who were actually fascinated.
2. People too stubborn to leave.
3. People clinging to their chicken-fried steak with sheer force of will.

By the end, the Optimist Club had become the Vegetarian Club, and I had officially ruined lunch for 100 civic leaders.

Dr. Peerwani, of course, was thrilled. "Thank you for being such a wonderful audience," he said, offering to come back anytime. The club president shook his hand warmly and replied, "That won't be necessary."

You'd think I would have learned. But no—my so-called *friends* in the younger crowd decided to "help me out." They swore the best program every year was a belly dancer. "It's a tradition," they said.

So I booked her. She quoted a $300 fee. I told them we had no budget. "Don't worry," they said, "we'll cover it."

Friday, 12:30.

The music started. She came out in full costume. And let's just say this was not your standard civic-club entertainment. Think less *cultural showcase* and more *strip-club matinee*, complete with near-lap dances and a waistband collection system.

My "friends" roared with laughter. The rest of the room? Horrified. By 1:00 p.m., my phone was buzzing with apologies and complaints—*Why would you bring that trash into First United Methodist?*

Turns out, there had never been a belly dancer before. It was a setup. The Medical Examiner had been bad. The Belly Dancer? A whole new category of bad.

I thought my reputation as Program Chair was permanently buried—until I finally redeemed myself years later.

Eddie Robinson, a former New York Yankee and several-time World Series Champion on two different teams, agreed to speak and brought along his friend Dr. Bobby Brown—also a Yankee, also a World Series champ, and at the time, President of the American League. These guys had stories: DiMaggio (Marilyn Monroe), Berra, the golden age of baseball. These two actually went on the first part of DiMaggio and Monroe's honeymoon in Hawaii, so DiMaggio would have someone to play golf with.

To avoid "dumb questions" like *What's your favorite song?*, Eddie and I came up with a plan. Members wrote their questions on slips of paper, I tossed them into a hat, and—miraculously—I only drew the ones Eddie and Dr. Brown wanted to answer.

That program not only salvaged my reputation, it kicked off a major campaign to support our Little League program. On opening day, both men showed up, threw out the first pitch, and made those kids feel like champions.

Take that, Belly Dance Boys.

23

1984: FROM MORTICIAN
TO DAD EXTRAORDINAIRE

Nineteen eighty-four didn't have the chaos of 1980, but it was no less life-changing.

For one, I completed my apprenticeship, marking the final step toward becoming fully licensed. All I had left was one more test—which, at that point, felt like a formality. The results came in: I'd passed. I was officially a Licensed Funeral Director and Embalmer. Or, if you prefer the more dramatic version: a Licensed Mortician.

And the big moment? Imagine a graduation ceremony—only at the DMV. No caps, no gowns, just a piece of paper slid across the counter, along with a cheerful reminder: *"Congratulations. Also, every two years, you'll need sixteen hours of continuing education."* So much for fanfare.

But the real headline of 1984 wasn't a funeral license. It was the birth of my son, **Jon David Thompson**.

We had a scheduled C-section, so I knew the exact time and day—but that didn't make it any less surreal. There I was, head to toe in scrubs, trying to look calm while also wondering how fast I could hit the floor if I fainted. The doctor worked a few minutes, then looked up and announced: *"It's a boy!"*

And just like that, everything changed.

My wife and I had a deal—she'd name a girl; I'd name a boy. I wanted a strong name. At first, I leaned toward John Paul Thompson. But then it hit me: I didn't want anyone thinking I was a die-hard Pope fan. Nothing against the man—but I didn't want my kid walking into a room and people whispering, *"Here comes the Pope."*

So, I settled on Jon—no "h"—inspired by two men who had shaped my life: Dr. Jon Fleming, president of Texas Wesleyan, and Jon Brumley, a kind and successful neighbor. For the middle name, I chose David. Why? It sounded good. It had zero papal associations. And it gave him an easy backup if he ever decided "Jon with no h" wasn't his thing.

Of course, that decision guaranteed him a lifetime of clarifying: *"Yes, Jon. No h. Really."* But it didn't matter. From the moment I saw him, my world shifted.

I had loved my Old English Sheepdog, Henry, like family. He'd been my companion, my sidekick, my confidant. But this? This was different. This was bigger. From that day forward, I knew I'd give my life for my son.

And something else happened in that hospital room. From that moment on, every child I ever cared for in the funeral home, I saw through the eyes of a father. It was no longer just work—it was personal. Each time, I thought of Jon. Each time, I asked myself: *What can I do to give this family my very best?*

That instinct started in 1984, and it has never left me. Nearly four decades later, I still feel that way today.

LESSONS FROM 1984

1. Graduation ceremonies are overrated—but licenses matter.

2. Never underestimate the politics of baby names.

3. A sheepdog may be man's best friend, but fatherhood changes

everything.

4. Being a dad made me a better funeral director—because every family deserved the same care I'd want for my own.

24

LEMON REALITY

The next few years of my life settled into a comfortable rhythm: wake up, shower, get dressed, and drive to work. Not exactly the plot of an action movie, but hey, I had upgraded from a station wagon to one of THC's Cadillac Broughams.

As I mentioned earlier, our entire fleet had been swapped out for dignified navy blue vehicles, a major improvement from the eye-searing pink rides we had before. I consider myself a secure man, but those pink funeral cars had been testing the limits of my masculinity.

My brother Vic chose to drive a Suburban, and we even replaced the old station wagon first-call cars with Suburbans too, which meant that Mom was finally spared the indignity of her old set of wheels.

Life was simple. Work was steady. Things were good.

And then, there was Christmas.

One December, Dad decided it was time to get Mom a new car. Dad wasn't exactly a car guy, but he had a certain way of describing things when he wanted something. That day, he casually mentioned, "She likes those cars that have numbers and letters on the back, you know?"

Numbers and letters?

"Yeah, something like a 500SL."

"Hold up, Dad—do you even know what that is?"

"I don't care. Just go find one."

So, off I went to the Mercedes dealership on the west side of Fort Worth, where I found it—a stunning white 500SL. It was sleek. It was luxurious. It was exactly the kind of car that screamed "I have arrived."

I called Dad to give him the good news.

"Have them wire Bank of Commerce for payment," he instructed.

"Dad . . . do you know how much these cars cost?"

"I'm sure it's somewhere around $10,000."

"No, Dad. It's $30,000."

Silence.

A long pause.

Then—

"Come straight back here."

And just like that, the dream of a numbers-and-letters car vanished.

Instead of a Mercedes 500SL, Mom ended up with a black Chrysler 5th Avenue. It wasn't exactly a status symbol, but at least it had words instead of numbers and letters, which I guess made it easier to spell.

The problem? It was a lemon. A sour, mechanical disaster that reminded us all that sometimes, numbers and letters actually mean something.

In the end, Mom got a new car—but Dad got a story that would live on forever.

And me? I learned never to let Dad go car shopping based on a hunch.

25

COACHING FIASCOS

Watching Jon grow from a movie-obsessed toddler to a sports-loving schoolboy was one of the greatest joys of my life. And my ill-fated coaching stints in various sports? Let's just say enthusiasm often trumped expertise.

Some of my best memories with Jon start with *Ghostbusters*. I rented the movie one night, thinking it would be a fun watch. What I didn't realize was that "Ghostbusters" would become the soundtrack of our household. The moment the credits rolled, Jon turned to me and said, "Let's watch it again!"

And so we did.

Over. And over. And over again.

At one point, I had rented it so many times that I probably could have paid for an entire Blockbuster franchise. Eventually, common sense prevailed, and I just bought the damn thing.

Jon didn't just watch *Ghostbusters*—he became one. He had his own Ghostbuster outfit, complete with a proton pack, which he wore every single day. Other clothes? Who needed them when you had a jumpsuit and a mission to bust ghosts?

At night, while he slept in his Ghostbuster pajamas, we would sneak his real Ghostbuster jumpsuit into the wash. By morning, it was clean, dry, and ready for another day of ghost-hunting. I loved every second of it.

By the time Jon turned four, signs went up all over the neighborhood announcing soccer sign-ups. On the appointed day, we strolled into the rec center, and the guy behind the table gave me some news. "All the teams are full, but we have a group of kids who want to play—if we can find a coach." At that moment, something deep inside me stirred. A forgotten dream. A calling from childhood.

I had once been destined to be a professional kickball player.

Soccer? That's basically just kickball with fancier rules, right?

So, I did what any overly confident and completely unqualified father would do. I volunteered to coach.

There was just one small problem: I knew absolutely nothing about soccer.

Growing up in Texas, soccer wasn't exactly a thing. Grade school? No soccer team. High school? No soccer team. College? No soccer team. Dallas even getting a professional team? Not for another eight years.

But I wasn't going to let that stop me. As with everything in my life, I turned to the library (well, after I finally stopped avoiding it, that is, and realized it was a treasure trove of information).

I checked out every book I could find on soccer and coaching. I studied for real, even memorizing all the fancy terms: Centering Kick. Angle of Run. Formation. Golazo. Bicycle Kick. Decoy Run. Back Heel Kick.

By the time our first practice rolled around, I was ready to mold these four-year-olds into a World Cup–caliber team. And then reality hit me like a rogue soccer ball to the face.

The first five minutes of practice were enough to tell me that I had wasted a whole lot of time preparing. There was no need for strategy. No need for formations, angles of attack, or fancy coaching lingo. I should have just relied on my kickball experience because seriously, all they needed to know was how to kick the ball. And if by some miracle, they kicked it in the right direction, that was a bonus.

Our first official game was a masterclass in controlled chaos. Most of the time, the kids just ran around aimlessly, occasionally colliding with each other, while the ball rolled around as an afterthought. When the other team miraculously managed to get the ball going toward our goal, I looked over at my goalkeeper to find him sitting in the grass, playing with weeds, completely oblivious to the game happening around him.

Needless to say, we didn't win that game.

Or the next one.

Or the one after that.

But none of that mattered because the kids had a blast.

And honestly? So did I.

When baseball sign-ups rolled around, the story was almost identical.

"We need a coach."

"Sure! I'll coach."

Did I know anything about coaching baseball?

No.

Did that stop me?

Not even a little.

Basketball? *Sure.*

Football? *Why not.*

At this point, I figured if enthusiasm was all it took to be a great coach, I was on my way to the Hall of Fame. But the real reason I kept saying yes had nothing to do with soccer, baseball, or any other sport. It had everything to do with Jon.

I wanted to be there—on the field, on the sidelines, in the

moments when he scored a goal, missed a shot, or just ran in circles for no reason at all.

Because that's what mattered.

And if coaching a sport I didn't understand meant spending more time with my son, then sign me up.

Again and again and again.

26

SHEAR GENIUS

B ecause, naturally, when you spend your days as a funeral director, the next logical step is to open a luxury hair salon.

It began when Jon's mother, Eleanor (spoiler alert: wife #1), a hairstylist with over twenty years of experience, started talking about needing a change. She and a fellow stylist were tired of their old salon in Hurst and looking for something better.

They weren't alone—a handful of other stylists were also itching for a fresh start.

Me? I smelled opportunity.

At the time, Colleyville was quickly becoming a hotspot for well-to-do families moving in from all over the country. It had the perfect mix of new money, big houses, and an ever-growing population of women with disposable income, plenty of free time, and husbands who traveled out of town Monday through Friday. In other words, a town full of women looking for something to do.

And we were about to give them exactly that. We didn't just want a salon—we wanted a destination. So we built one with eighteen chairs, each leased to a stylist; two nail stations; and five shampoo ladies. With twenty-five women working under one roof, it was always lively, to say the least. And each stylist was her own boss who set her own schedule, while we handled the bookings and provided flexible shampoo assistance. It was a win-win for everyone.

In short order, the salon became the place to be.

Every time I dropped by—usually at night to help with ordering products or fixing whatever needed fixing—it was buzzing with energy. And let's just say, those stylists knew how to let their hair down. (Yes, pun intended.) We even threw some legendary pool parties, where I quickly learned that hairstylists were just as fun outside of work as they were inside it.

Now, here's the part I didn't see coming. Owning a salon meant having wholesale access to salon-quality beauty products. And what does a funeral home also require? Salon-quality beauty products. Suddenly, THC had a stockpile of top-notch cosmetics, nail polishes, shampoos, and rinses.

Our dearly departed had never looked better.

I had officially turned a side business into a funeral home perk.

Call it shear genius if I do say so myself.

27

FROM FUNERAL CONVENTIONS
TO ROCKPORT MISADVENTURES

While other kids were off to Disneyland or camping trips, our family was heading to the Texas Funeral Directors Association (TFDA) convention. Because what's more exciting for a kid than spending a summer surrounded by caskets, hearses, and embalming fluid demonstrations?

Our usual home base for the convention was the historic Menger Hotel in San Antonio, conveniently located right next to the Alamo. On paper, it had everything: a cool indoor pool where we could splash around, a parrot in the lobby with a surprisingly colorful vocabulary, and history! (Though when you grow up in funeral service, "history" tends to mean *lots of stories about dead people*.)

But let's be honest—funeral conventions aren't exactly Disneyland.

So, when we weren't swimming or trying to teach the Menger's parrot new words it definitely shouldn't know, we'd wander the exhibition hall—a place that was basically a twisted version of a carnival. Instead of cotton candy and Ferris wheels, we had casket vendors, vault vendors, and funeral car vendors. Each one handed out goodies, so we'd fill our bags with candy, toys, and trinkets—except for the one item we knew better than to bring home: the dreaded paddleball toy.

Sure, it was fun for about five minutes, but Mom always confiscated it before long. Why? Because in her hands, it ceased to be a toy and became her new favorite discipline tool.

By the time I had kids of my own, I decided to give them a different kind of summer vacation experience. So, by the 1980s, we started heading to South Padre Island, where there were no funeral conventions, no caskets, and no paddleball weapons. Just sand, sun, and seafood.

I still had my limousine, which was basically a rolling entertainment center. In the back, it converted into a cozy bed, and I'd load up on movies for the kids before the long drive. Not that it mattered—Jon only ever wanted to watch *Ghostbusters*.

Every summer, at 4 a.m. sharp, we'd hit the road for the ten-hour drive while the kids slept peacefully in the back. By the time they woke up, we'd be pulling into paradise.

Those trips were bliss-filled days of sunny beaches, great restaurants, no on-call duties, and best of all, no funeral homes.

Toward the end of the '80s, my brother Vic came up with an idea: instead of South Padre, why not Rockport? He had purchased a condo there, but unlike South Padre, Rockport wasn't exactly a beach town. It was on the water, though, and the condo sat on a canal that flowed into the bay. Plus, it was half the distance from Fort Worth, which sounded like a win to me.

One summer, we decided to test it out by bringing along my father-in-law, an avid fisherman, along with our trusty fishing boat. Rockport had a reputation as a fishing paradise, and we were ready to see if it lived up to the hype.

We spotted an island surrounded by fishing boats, and Jon,

my father-in-law, and I took off in our bass boat at full speed, straight toward it. Because, really, what could go wrong?

Well, turns out—a lot.

I soon learned the hard way that Rockport isn't just a name. It's a warning. Unbeknownst to us, there was a manmade channel for boats to safely navigate the area. And if you strayed from that channel? You'd meet the barnacle-covered rocks hiding just twelve inches below the surface.

Which is exactly what we did.

The other boats? They were Boston Whalers with a six-inch draft. Perfect for skimming over the rocks.

Our boat? Not so much.

Rock meets propeller.

Propeller loses.

We limped back to shore, a little humbler and a lot quieter. And that's when it hit me. While I may have successfully escaped the funeral conventions of my childhood, I hadn't quite escaped life's little lessons—like knowing when to steer clear of rock-strewn waters, both literal and metaphorical.

28

FROM FAIRWAY TO FLEEING: THE GREAT CLUB SWITCH OF '88

By the late '80s, Woodhaven was changing, and not for the better.

One afternoon, as I was heading to my car after a round, I noticed two young men pulling into the parking lot in a car that definitely didn't scream "member's kid." The duo didn't look familiar, and they certainly didn't look like they were there for a leisurely round of golf.

I got a bad feeling, so I picked up my pace and quickly jumped into my car, locking the doors. Unfortunately, another guy—just a few cars down from me—wasn't so lucky. Before he could even react, the passenger of the suspicious car rolled down his window, stuck a gun out, and robbed him right there in the parking lot. Afterward, they sped off like it was just another day at the office.

I bolted into the pro shop, where I found the victim already telling Mike Duggar, the club pro, what had just happened. As he was describing his traumatic encounter, another member burst through the doors and said he had just been robbed while walking off the third green.

Clearly, this wasn't just a one-off incident—this was becoming a pattern. And I wasn't the only one taking notice.

Over the next few weeks, more members had similar stories of cars broken into, golfers getting mugged mid-round, and guys with guns treating the course like an ATM.

Enough was enough.

A group of us decided it was time to find a safer place to play—preferably one where you didn't have to look over your shoulder between holes.

Ridglea Country Club had been one of my top choices for a while, and this was the push I needed to finally make the switch. Unlike Woodhaven, Ridglea had two golf courses, a strong membership, and—most importantly—a total lack of armed robberies on the fairways. Although they didn't have a formal gangsome, it wasn't long before we found a great group of guys to play with.

Ridglea wasn't just a safer choice for golf—it also became THC's go-to spot for hosting receptions and dinners after services. Getting involved with committees and new golf groups gave me an opportunity to spread our brand while enjoying a safer, more relaxed environment.

It was a win-win.

It did, however, come with one minor challenge.

Somewhere along the way, word got out that I had once—*once*—worn pink shorts on the golf course. And in golf circles, nicknames stick like glue—especially the embarrassing ones. For a brief moment, I was at serious risk of becoming "The Pink Flamingo." But I played it smart. I laughed along just enough to let them have their fun, then swiftly steered the conversation elsewhere.

Whew. Crisis averted.

Moving to Ridglea wasn't just about better golf—it was about peace of mind. Sure, Woodhaven had been a great club for years, but when your midweek round starts feeling like a crime documentary, it's time to pack up and go.

Luckily, at Ridglea, I not only had new golf buddies, but a

great club for THC's events with zero risk of getting mugged between shots. And honestly, that last one alone made the switch worth it.

29

GHOSTS, BIRDS, AND A TRAILBLAZING APPRENTICE

Thompson's Harveson & Cole has always been home to a colorful cast of employees, each bringing their own quirks, loyalties, and peculiar habits to the funeral business. Some of them stuck around for thirty, forty, even fifty years, becoming as much a part of the place as the old building itself.

If you asked any past or present THC employee to name the most memorable characters, you'd get a long list of personalities—each with their own unforgettable moments.

First, there was Leo, a man whose loyalty ran so deep that his entire family felt like they were part of the company, too.

Then there was Ed—a guy whose quirky sense of humor always surfaced at the most inappropriate, yet oddly perfect, moments.

Burt was another forty-plus-year veteran, but he was a ghost outside of work. No one ever saw his home, and as far as we knew, he didn't socialize with anyone after hours.

Frank, a retired anchorman from Channel 5, was our front-desk man. He was the first person to ever broadcast a live event for the station, and yet somehow, his voice had lost all its TV charm by the time he was buzzing me on the intercom.

And then there was Roger, the birdman—a guy who, no matter the request, never said no to me, my sister, or my dad.

Each of them added to the fabric of THC, making it not just a funeral home, but a place where loyalty, hard work, and the occasional bizarre story lived on.

One random day in 1988, I got a buzz from Frank at the front desk. His voice, more gruff than ever, crackled through the intercom:

"There's a girl up here looking for a funeral director job."

That was unusual. Women in funeral service were still rare at the time, and it was even rarer for one to walk in off the street asking for a job cold. Curious, I headed to the front, where I met a young woman with an air of quiet determination. She launched into her story, and within minutes, I was absolutely floored.

She had grown up dirt poor in El Paso and had hitchhiked to Dallas just to attend the newly renamed Dallas Institute of Funeral Service (DIFS). Her family support plan fell through, leaving her sleeping wherever she could. Eventually, another student took her in, allowing her to stay long enough to excel in school—despite every challenge stacked against her. Now, diploma in hand, she was determined to get her foot in the funeral industry. Every funeral home in Dallas and Fort Worth had turned her down. THC was her last hope before hitchhiking back to El Paso.

As luck would have it, we were looking for an apprentice. And after hearing her story, I felt a gut-punch of emotions. This was exactly the kind of person we needed—driven, hardworking, and committed.

I told her to wait there and went straight to my brother Vic, excited.

"I found someone for the job," I said.

"Hire him," Vic replied without even looking up.

"Well . . . it's actually a she," I corrected.

That got his attention.

Not only was she a woman, but she was Hispanic—which, at the time, we had never had before. There was a long pause. I could tell Vic was hesitant, but I also knew he wasn't someone who ignored talent when he saw it.

"Just meet her," I insisted.

So Vic sat down with her, and before long, I could tell he was as moved as I was. She had the drive, the resilience, and the intelligence—all she needed was a chance. That meant there was only one last hurdle: Dad.

Vic and I went to him together.

"Dad, we've got a great candidate for the apprentice position," we started.

"Hire him," Dad said.

"Actually, Dad, it's a her," I clarified.

He raised an eyebrow.

Vic and I told him her story, emphasizing how every other funeral home had turned her away. Dad listened in silence, nodded, and after a brief pause, simply said, "Hire her."

That day, Sylvia became part of THC.

Over the next twenty-plus years, she would go on to become one of Dad's all-time favorite hires.

Her story, a testament to resilience, became one of those legendary tales we'd tell whenever people asked how she got her start. It just goes to show that sometimes, the best hires don't come from polished résumés or fancy connections. Sometimes they walk in off the street with nothing but determination—and a story that needs a chance to be heard.

Part 5

THE TURNING POINT:

LIFE AFTER LOSS
AND A NEW BEGINNING

30

APRIL FOOLS AND DIVORCE BLUES

That morning, the day had started like any other birthday. Maybe a few phone calls, a joke or two about getting older, and the usual shuffle of work at the funeral home. Then the phone rang.

On the other end of the line was a man with a familiar voice.

"Mr. Thompson, you took care of my mom a few months ago. I need to serve you some papers and don't want to embarrass you in front of others. Can we do this in private?"

I paused.

Papers? Not wanting to embarrass me?

My brain worked through the possibilities, but before I could fully process what was happening, I told him to meet me at my office behind the funeral home. Minutes later, he arrived, papers in hand.

I opened the envelope, scanned the contents, and felt a wave of irony wash over me.

Divorce papers.

On my birthday.

From a guy whose family I had helped just months before.

He looked at me, genuinely apologetic. "I'm really sorry about this," he said, as if that somehow made the situation better.

I nodded, let out a small laugh—because what else can you do?—and said, "Well, at least I won't forget the anniversary of this one."

Happy birthday to me.

Time for a fresh start.

31

HONEYMOON SURPRISES

One of the must-attend events in Fort Worth is the Colonial National Invitational Golf Tournament. It's a tradition, a spectacle, and a social event where you're just as likely to run into an old friend as you are to brush shoulders with golf legends.

Wednesday is Pro-Am Day, and if you really want to be in the middle of it all, you head straight to the Terrace Room above the 18th hole. It's always packed wall to wall, buzzing with conversation, drinks flowing, and, if you're lucky, a few unexpected encounters.

That's exactly what happened to me that night.

I was newly single, still adjusting to my fresh divorce papers, and not exactly on the lookout for love. But then I met Janice.

We struck up a conversation, exchanged numbers, and before I even had time to second-guess myself, I called her a few days later. Her response?

"My friend and I joked it would be the undertaker who called first."

I wasn't sure if that was a compliment or a warning—but either way, I wasn't about to let it slide.

That first date led to another, and then another. She was beautiful, successful, and had a great sense of humor. And while

I'd love to say she was immediately smitten, the true test came with her dogs. Lucky for me, they didn't try to bite me.

By September, my divorce was finalized, and Janice and I were having lunch when, in what could only be described as a remarkably unromantic proposal, I said, "You know we're probably going to get married, so we may as well do it."

Smooth, right?

To my surprise, she agreed.

Her only condition? "It should be before Thanksgiving or after New Year's."

We went with before Thanksgiving.

We both wanted something small, intimate, and simple—a short and sweet ceremony at the First Presbyterian Church chapel with Dr. Bohl, a good friend, officiating. But when we arrived, the chapel was packed. Not only that—some guests were even standing outside.

Dr. Bohl, who loved an audience, took this as his moment to shine. Our "short and sweet" service suddenly had a bit more flair and length, but it was absolutely perfect. On November 14, 1992, I became the luckiest man alive when Janice said "I do."

Planning a honeymoon on short notice, however, didn't leave us with many options. After some scrambling, we booked a cruise departing from San Juan, stopping at Aruba, Curaçao, Virgin Gorda, St. Thomas, and then back to San Juan. Sounded perfect!

Then we saw the ship: it was old, small, and definitely on the verge of retirement. But it was our honeymoon, so we decided to make the best of it.

After an amazing dinner, we found ourselves at bingo night—not exactly something I'd planned, but hey, why not? The last game of the night was blackout bingo, with a solid jackpot of $1,000. And guess what? I won.

That win led to the next big gamble of the trip.

They were auctioning off five wooden horses for a horse race on the last night of the cruise. The idea was simple—each "horse owner" would name their horse, decorate it, and spend the week convincing other passengers to place bets on it. Since I had just won a thousand bucks, I figured—why not? I bought a horse, and Janice and I named him Big Tex.

Since Janice is a proud University of Texas alum, we painted him burnt orange and gave him a full Longhorns theme. Big Tex was instantly a crowd favorite, and we made friends with people all over the ship. By midweek, we couldn't walk into a bar without drinks already waiting for us, and the crew treated us like VIPs.

On the last night, the betting odds were posted—Big Tex had the lowest payout because he was the favorite to win. So, naturally . . .

I bet on another horse.

Well, turns out Big Tex lost. So did my bet.

But at the end of the day—who cared?

We had the time of our lives, met incredible people, and added some of our favorite destinations to our list for future trips.

It may not have been a luxury cruise, and we may have lost our bet—but it was our honeymoon, and nothing was going to put a damper on it.

32

COWBOYS AND COCKTAILS

f life has taught me anything, it's that sometimes you sign up for a golf tournament and end up in a cowboy-filled hotel where the boots are high, the hats are wide, and the PDA is . . . unexpectedly enthusiastic.

I had gotten deeply involved in the Optimist Club, rarely missing a weekly luncheon. What started as attending meetings turned into chairing the golf tournament—which, honestly, felt like the perfect fit for me.

My dad always said he was never much of a "joiner," but I knew that one of us needed to be out in the community for THC. Besides the Optimist Club, I had also joined the board of the Arthritis Foundation, where I helped organize their annual charity golf tournament with a rather infamous baseball player, Bobby Bragan. Bobby was a legend, and not just for baseball. He was a born entertainer, and every civic club that needed a program speaker had him on speed dial, because if you needed someone who could work a room, Bobby was your guy.

I had just wrapped up my second year of working with Bobby on the Arthritis Foundation golf tournament, and things were going extremely well. We had brought in nearly $100,000 in revenue, and we spent almost all of it on prizes, players, and the celebrities Bobby brought in.

It was one of the biggest charity golf events in the area.

One year, I played in the tournament with Eddie Robinson, and during a lull in conversation, he turned to me and said, "You know, we have a lot of Major League Baseball alumni living in the area. It would be great if we could have a tournament involving them and a local charity."

That was Eddie's big heart. He was heavily involved in the Major League Baseball Players Alumni Association (MLBPAA), and he knew firsthand the struggles that retired players faced. While today's players were making millions, and pensions would eventually take care of them, his generation had no pensions, no multi-million-dollar contracts, and no safety net. Many of his old teammates were living on next to nothing, some in Medicaid-supported nursing homes that were far from luxurious. He wanted to raise money to help these former ballplayers with their basic needs—and that's when it hit me.

"Eddie," I said, "my Optimist Club needs a boost for our charity golf tournament, and our biggest program is a Little League baseball organization for disadvantaged kids." I saw it as a perfect match—we could raise money for both the MLBPAA players and the kids' baseball league.

Eddie was game, so we took the idea to MLBPAA headquarters in St. Pete Beach, FL, and soon other alumni in different cities were launching their own tournaments. By the time we really hit our stride, we had national sponsors on board for our tournament and all the others across the country.

Eddie wanted to bring in executives from our national sponsors—companies like Rolaids, American Tourister, and others. Each company donated $5,000 to the cause at each tournament, and by then, we had over twenty tournaments around the country. So, to kick things off properly, I booked a suite at the Hilton Hotel in downtown Fort Worth for a private cocktail party. We flew in the top executives, some Hall of Famers, and put everyone up at the Hilton. Everything was going according to plan, until my wife and I arrived at the Hilton midday to set up the suite.

Apparently, the Hilton was also hosting a very different kind of event that weekend.

The National Gay Rodeo.

Now, we were expecting to see cowboys in Texas; we just weren't expecting to see them kissing each other in the hotel lobby. To say it was a surprise would be an understatement. These cowboys weren't just dressed to the nines—they had bedazzled everything that could be bedazzled and were wearing chaps that probably cost more than my first car. And they weren't shy about their affection for one another.

That night, at our executive cocktail party, let's just say it made for some . . . interesting conversation. Most of our guests agreed.

Yes, they had expected to see cowboys in Texas.

No, they hadn't expected this particular variety.

But despite the unexpected rodeo subplot, the event was a huge success. The sponsors were thrilled, the tournament was set up for a record-breaking year, and our cause was gaining serious momentum.

And the Gay Rodeo Cowboys?

Well, let's just say they knew how to throw a party too.

33

SCOUTING SHENANIGANS

We enrolled Jon in Hill School, a fantastic institution that not only focused on academics but also offered plenty of sports.

On his very first day, he made instant friends and quickly discovered he was a natural athlete: basketball, baseball, football—you name it, Jon played it, and played it well. I'd like to think he got it from me, but considering my athletic peak was kickball champion of my elementary school, I think we'll chalk it up to natural talent.

As much as I enjoyed watching Jon play sports, I had another father-son bonding idea: Cub Scouts. I loved scouting when I was a kid, and convincing Jon to join was my excuse to relive my glory days.

Since I knew all the best camping spots, we booked trips at the same places I had camped back in my youth. That summer, we signed up for the big camp at Leonard Scout Campground, where my scouting nostalgia came crashing headfirst into reality.

At first, things were going great. We had a solid plan, and three other dads agreed to be chaperones for the weekend. But as parents were dropping off their kids, each of the three came up to me with the same guilty look and said, "I'm sorry, but something came up and I can't stay."

And just like that . . . I was the lone adult responsible for twelve eight-year-olds.

In the pitch-black woods.

With kids who had never been away from home before.

It wasn't exactly what I had signed up for, but I tried my best to keep things organized.

First order of business? *Survival.*

I set up a chair in the center of our tent circle, armed with a flashlight, ready to fight off both wild animals and homesickness meltdowns. Before lights out, I warned the kids: "Do NOT keep food in your tents. The possums here have a major sweet tooth."

The first few hours were surprisingly peaceful, but at 2 a.m., the screaming started when one tent erupted in chaos with shouts of "THERE'S A BEAR INSIDE!"

Now, I had already seen their so-called bear leaving the tent— and unless bears had recently shrunk to the size of a housecat and grown a long, rat-like tail, this was a possum. Still, the kids were panicked, so I got them to do what any rational scout leader would: cough up all their candy and treats so we could go back to sleep.

Out came half-melted chocolate bars, sticky gum, and partially eaten bags of Skittles, which I tossed out far, far away from camp.

Possum crisis averted.

The next morning, I was reminded of one key thing I had completely forgotten about scout camps: no warm running water. The showers weren't just cold—they felt like a punishment.

By day three, I was convinced I had somehow disrespected the spirits of scouting past, and this was their way of teaching me a lesson in humility. So I gritted my teeth, made it through the week, and Jon and I both came to the same conclusion: scouting just wasn't our thing.

Though, honestly, I wouldn't have minded sticking with it a little longer (as long as someone else took possum patrol duty).

34

FARM LIFE AND
COSMIC COINCIDENCES

Janice's parents' home was on what they called a "farm," but that word was a bit misleading. They didn't actually farm anything. Instead, they had two sprawling properties:

1) The Main Property – Home to the main house, large pastures, two ponds, a hay barn, an outbuilding with workout equipment, and a shed for farm equipment.

2) The Second Property – Mostly pasture and trees, also with two ponds, perfect for cows to wade in and city folks like me to stare at in admiration.

Now, before we headed out there for the first time, Janice gave me a heads-up.

"They might look at you a little funny," she said. And then she explained why.

Many years before, Janice's little brother, John Martin Furry, had passed away when he was a little younger than Jon was now. And now, here she was, bringing home a Jon and a Martin. Talk about a cosmic coincidence. It was one of those moments that made you stop and wonder if the universe was playing some kind of inside joke.

But if first impressions were an Olympic sport, Myrl and Fawn Furry would have taken the gold medal for kindness. They were two of the warmest, most gentle people I had ever met. Don't let that fool you, though. Myrl was as sharp as they come. He ran a cow/calf operation and had his own oil and gas production company.

The moment we arrived, he handed Jon and me an invitation we couldn't refuse: "Hop in the truck, boys. Let's take a ride."

And just like that, we were off on a grand tour of the farm/ranch.

Now, let's be clear—growing up in Texas doesn't mean you automatically know how to wrangle cattle. Most people assume we all live on ranches, ride horses to school, and have boots permanently attached to our feet. But I grew up in Fort Worth, which made me a city boy through and through. Yet, here I was, riding shotgun as Myrl checked on cows, threw hay bales, mended fences, and tended to his oil leases.

It didn't take me long to realize I needed a good pair of leather gloves because well, this was real work. Jon, on the other hand, had his own set of discoveries. At one point, he wrinkled his nose and complained about the strong smell around the pump jacks. Myrl just chuckled.

"No, Jon. This smells really good."

Only an oil man could appreciate the sweet scent of crude.

During those rides, Myrl and I bonded over everything. He told me stories about growing up dirt poor in a tiny Texas town called Groves Venner (actually spelled Grovesnor), north of Brownwood. Later, he took me out to see it. The whole town was basically abandoned—nothing but empty buildings and memories.

Myrl also shared stories of his time in World War II. When the Army drafted him, they put him on a train packed with recruits, sending them crisscrossing Texas for an entire day—only for Myrl to end up in Abilene, just a hundred miles from Brown-wood. In other words, a long trip to go nowhere. After boot camp, he was shipped to England to prepare for D-Day, where he found a creative way to avoid seasickness—staying on deck the entire time.

My mother-in-law, Fawn, grew up even poorer than Myrl in a town called Cross Cut. After raising her family, she went back to school and became a teacher—a job she loved and kept for years. She was small in stature, but she had a quiet strength that held everything together.

Despite their hardships, Myrl and Fawn never lost their love for baseball, especially the Texas Rangers. It became our daily ritual to call each other during games, either to gloat over a great play or complain about a terrible one.

Thanks to my friendship with Eddie Robinson and our MLB-PA golf tournament, I got to bring Myrl along to meet some of his baseball heroes. Those moments were priceless.

For Myrl and Fawn, family was everything. From the very first visit, they took Jon and me in as their own. And for that, I will always be grateful.

35

FUNERAL HOME ADVENTURES

The funeral home was thriving. Dad, Vic, and I would meet with families and work funerals together, running THC like a well-oiled machine. Janice and I traveled often, making it a priority to take at least two trips a year—one domestic, one international. We had a great group of friends, some of whom even joined us on our adventures. And finally, after years of playing musical golf clubs, I joined River Crest, the top club on my list.

Meanwhile, Jon was excelling in school—not only academically, but athletically, earning Athlete of the Year twice.

Everything was running smoothly. And then, I arranged one of the most unforgettable funeral services of my career.

Dad had gone up to Syracuse for his annual buying trip and Vic was at his place in Rockport, which meant that I was manning the fort. At 5:30 a.m., the funeral home phone rang, and the family name was one I knew well. I went to the hospital with one of our team members, where the deceased's son was already waiting. He was gracious, well-spoken, and we chatted for a while. Then, as the conversation shifted, I asked the usual question: "Would you like us to bring our cot in to receive your mother?"

His response? "Can I help?"

I hesitated. Not a common request, but I nodded. "Sure."

As we carefully placed his mother on the cot, I noticed something. He wasn't ready to leave. He walked with us to the elevator, then out to the car. Then, he followed us all the way back to the funeral home. Along the way, he kept saying the same thing. "I just can't imagine seeing my mother in a casket."

Now, after years in funeral service, you learn to listen. So I paused, considered his words, and offered an alternative.

"If that would be difficult for you, we could place her in a bed for the viewing."

His face lit up. "Could we?"

"Of course."

He paused briefly. "Could we use her actual bed?"

Again, not a typical request, but again, I nodded. "Absolutely."

And just like that, a simple funeral arrangement turned into something entirely unique.

Over the next few days, we transformed a visitation room into a perfect re-creation of her bedroom. The bed. The nightstand. The chairs. The bric-a-brac. Every last detail. But that was just the beginning.

The family decided on a Saturday night service at Broadway Baptist—because Saturday night was "prime time" for the son. So, we pulled out all the stops in the form of:

+ A 200-piece orchestra made up of the first strings from the Fort Worth Symphony, Dallas Symphony, Houston Symphony, and Austin Symphony

+ A 200-plus member choir

+ Music commissioned specifically for the service

+ 18 limousines to transport family and close friends, complete with a meticulously detailed car list

+ Floral arrangements unlike anything I had ever seen

Dad cut his trip short and high-tailed it back to Texas.

On the night of the service, I had all eighteen limousines staged at the funeral home. Every available Fort Worth motor officer was there to escort us, and we even hired five additional ones. From the home, to the church, and back, it was a sight to behold. And then came the eulogy.

It was delivered by Paul Harvey—yes, *that* Paul Harvey—to a church packed with dignitaries from all over the country.

The orchestra played flawlessly.

The choir was magnificent.

Everything unfolded with absolute perfection.

It was, without a doubt, one of the most elaborate and breathtaking services I have ever been part of.

At the end of the service, our ten hired pallbearers shouldered the 3" Plank Mahogany Marcellus Masterpiece casket and carried her out.

As I drove the son and his closest friends, I turned to him and asked, "Was everything as you hoped?"

He looked out the window for a moment, then turned to me and smiled.

And then he said something I will never forget.

"That service was perfect. It wasn't ostentatious at all."

I nearly laughed.

Two hundred musicians. Eighteen limousines. A church packed with dignitaries. Paul Harvey himself delivering the eulogy.

Not ostentatious at all.

But in that moment, I realized something. For him, it truly wasn't ostentatious. It was simply what his mother deserved.

And in the end, that's all that really mattered.

36

VIC'S LAST LAUGH

I t was mid-December of 1994 when Vic started experiencing serious health issues.

Vic was larger than life—the kind of guy everyone loved, admired, and never forgot. He was my older brother, my idol, and one of the funniest, most charismatic people I had ever known. Even now, thirty years later, people still come up to me and share stories about him, their faces lighting up as if he had just walked into the room.

He and his wife, Carla, married right out of Texas Wesleyan, where she also attended. They had three incredible boys—Theo, Tim, and Trent—who have grown into outstanding men, carrying their father's warmth, humor, and kindness with them.

At first, Vic brushed off how he was feeling. He still came to work, but something wasn't right.

On Monday, he called in sick.

On Tuesday, he called in again.

By Thursday, Dad got worried—and Dad wasn't the type to panic.

Before he was a funeral director, Dad had been a Chief Pharmacist's Mate in the Navy—a man who had seen everything, treated everything, and didn't let much shake him. But this time?

Dad went to check on Vic and, ever the practical one, suggested that he go to the hospital for an IV. The next day, Vic seemed better. He was cracking jokes, entertaining a steady stream of visitors, and being his usual self. It was a relief and we all let out a breath. Maybe it was just a bad flu, after all.

But on Saturday, December 18th, my mother was carrying on our long-standing Christmas tradition—taking the grandkids to see a holiday movie—when my brother Tim, a priest, walked into the theater. "Thompson family," he announced, "come out to the lobby."

The moment we saw Tim's face, our hearts dropped. He told us Vic had taken a turn for the worse and that we needed to get to the hospital right away. So we rushed to All Saints, where they had set up a family room for us.

When Vic's doctor came in, his face was solemn. "His system is shutting down," he said.

I felt like the air had been knocked out of my chest. Just yesterday, he had been joking and laughing, and now, we were being told there was nothing more they could do.

We each went in, one by one, to say goodbye.

That night, around 2 a.m., Vic passed away.

And suddenly, we were planning a funeral we never wanted to plan.

I had always assumed that Dad—who had spent his entire career comforting grieving families—would be stoic, strong, unshakable. And I had assumed that Mom—deeply faithful, always praying her rosary—would grieve openly, emotionally, and without hesitation.

But grief doesn't follow expectations.

Dad—the rock, the strong one, the one who never wavered—grieved openly. More than I ever expected. And Mom, who had always worn her heart on her sleeve, kept a stiff upper lip, showing no emotion at all.

Over time, their grief took two completely different paths.

Dad allowed himself to remember Vic. He talked about him, shared stories, laughed about the past. He grieved . . . and then he celebrated his son.

Mom, though . . . she never spoke his name again. If someone mentioned Vic in conversation, she would quietly leave the room. She never cried in front of us. She never reminisced. She held it all inside. I truly believe she silently grieved his loss for the rest of her life.

Even in his passing, Vic had a way of leaving a mark. At the funeral, friends, colleagues, and family filled the chapel. The stories people told, the laughter through the tears—it was all Vic. He had a way of bringing people together, of making them feel like they belonged, like they mattered. That was his gift.

And it's a gift that never faded.

I miss you, Vic.

Even now, all these years later—I miss him.

I miss his humor. I miss his wisdom. I miss his presence.

But more than anything, I miss my big brother.

37

THE TURNING POINT

The mood in our family shifted like a storm rolling in, gradual at first, then suddenly impossible to ignore. Grief didn't just touch us—it consumed us. And in a family business, where personal and professional lives are already intertwined, it felt like we were trying to keep a ship afloat in rough seas, with no captain.

Looking back, I realize now that—just like my mother—I never allowed myself the time or space to truly grieve. Instead, I did what so many of us do. I put my head down and kept moving forward. We all did. We put on brave faces, tried to act normal, and went through the motions. But deep down, we were anything but normal.

And the business? It felt off.

The steady rhythm of Harveson & Cole had turned into a dissonant tune, a vibe the people around us felt, too. Long-time employees—people who had been with us for decades—started leaving. Some retired, some moved on. And some just needed a fresh start.

Honestly? I couldn't blame them. The foundation we had built over the years felt unsteady, and even I was starting to wonder: was I holding on too tightly to something that no longer fit?

By 1998, I had been at Harveson & Cole for twenty-two years, and I knew deep in my gut that it was time for a change. The chapter was closing, and as much as I wanted to force things back to the way they were, I couldn't. I was done trying to hold together something that wasn't meant to stay the same.

It was time to turn the page and see what came next.

38

FROM TEE TIME
TO FUNERAL HOME

At forty, I had a startling realization: after a lifetime of working (or, let's be honest, hanging around) Thompson's Harveson & Cole, I was officially unemployed and directionless. For the first time, I had to ask myself: What now?

At first, things were pretty sweet. I was living the dream, spending my days playing in golf gangsomes at River Crest. Every morning, my wife would ask, "What are you going to do today?" and my answer was always the same: "I'm going to play in the gangsome." Life was good.

Then came the lists. "Before you go, could you do this?" became "this and that," and before I knew it, I was buried under "this, that, and every damn thing." When my pre-golf to-do list started cutting into my tee time, I knew it was time to get a job.

And what was I good at? Funeral directing, of course. But since I had sold my interest in the funeral home, I had a non-compete clause that wrapped around Loop 820 like a noose, meaning if I wanted to open my own place, I had to venture beyond the loop.

Around that time, I caught wind of a rumor—the most successful funeral home in Weatherford was about to sell to SCI, the funeral home behemoth. Competing with a corporate funeral home? Easy. They're overpriced and they under-serve, so I figured I'd have the market in no time.

A few days later, my friend Roger Williams invited me to lunch and a tour of some properties in Weatherford. Just as I was picturing my grand Weatherford takeover, I got the news: the rumor was just that—a rumor. The top funeral home wasn't selling after all. Competing against a well-run, family-owned funeral home wasn't my style, so it was back to square one.

I turned to Janice and said, "It's time to hit the mid-cities."

The next day, I started driving around Keller, Southlake, Colleyville, and Grapevine, scouting out communities and buildings. Late in the day, I called Janice and declared, "It's got to be Grapevine. This town has a unique charm, great properties, and just the right vibe. Tomorrow, I'm calling our real estate agent to start looking for available properties."

Just as I was saying this, I happened upon a three-story Victorian house, built in 1888, with a For Lease sign out front. I pulled over and told Janice, "I just found our funeral home."

"What?" she said, probably thinking I'd lost my mind.

"I just pulled up in front of the perfect place. Let me call you back."

I got out and did a quick walk around the house—known as the Dorris House—and immediately knew this was it.

The next day, Janice and I toured the place, and before long, we put a contract on it. The outside was nearly perfect, with only a few minor cosmetic changes needed, but the inside? Let's just say it needed a lot of love.

Dad's funeral home was always immaculate, even though it was just as old as this place, so I knew what could be done. I hired an interior decorator and a contractor and jumped headfirst into a major renovation project. The walls had more cracks than a plumber's convention, but that didn't deter me. I even found a piece of the original 1888 wallpaper in a closet on the second floor and had the pattern copied. Then, I took it to a fabric store to get matching or complementary drapes and wall coverings.

I spent months combing through antique stores for period-appropriate furniture for the Victorian home—only to realize later that Victorian folks were a lot smaller than modern-day, well-padded people, and their furniture wasn't exactly built for comfort. I designed logos and themes with a period flair, and as the renovations wrapped up, the *Grapevine Sun* came down to do a feature piece on the new funeral home.

But here's where things got a little weird.

One night during the renovation, I was working late on the third floor, which I planned to use as my office and, occasionally, a bedroom. My phone system had a feature where you could press the speaker button and it would activate the dial tone. The house had a spiral staircase that went from the third floor all the way down to the first, so you could hear everything echoing up and down.

Suddenly, that all-too-familiar electronic hum filled the air—not from my phone, but from the one downstairs. My stomach tightened. I was alone. Or so I thought.

I went down, turned it off, and figured my contractor was playing a prank. But when I couldn't find him—or his truck—I went back upstairs. A few minutes later, the speaker button activated again downstairs.

This time, I knew something was up. I went down, and the phone was on again. But no contractor, no prankster—just me and that creepy house.

By the third time, every hair on my body was at full attention. If ghosts are real, this one clearly had a thing for long-distance calls.

Anyway, back to the renovations.

The Sunday before our grand opening, the *Grapevine Sun* published their feature piece, including an interview with long-time mayor William D. Tate. They asked him what he thought about the Dorris House becoming Martin Thompson Funeral Home.

His response?

"Grapevine already has two funeral homes that have been here for over a hundred years each, so I don't think Grapevine needs another funeral home. I wish the Dorris House had stayed a restaurant."

I looked at my wife and said, "Well, I don't think I'm getting a key to the city anytime soon. Guess I'll stick to burying people instead of winning them over."

39

FROM REMODEL TO ROLL CALL:
THE GRAPEVINE GAMBLE

Transforming the Dorris House into a funeral home was a leap of faith. Armed with a DIY advertising binder and sheer determination, we opened our doors—unsure if anyone would actually walk through them.

We wrapped up the remodeling in December 1998, and I called the Texas Funeral Service Commission to schedule an inspection. Their response?

"We can get to you in about a month."

A month? Sure, why not? I was already opening a funeral home in a town where no one knew me, with two existing funeral homes that had been around since the dinosaurs (or at least the mayor made it sound that way). What was another month of waiting?

The only time I had ever set foot in Grapevine was to play golf. I knew nobody. No local connections, no word-of-mouth referrals, no built-in clientele. And unlike Thompson's Harveson & Cole, where we had a solid reputation and didn't need to advertise, I now had no choice but to market myself.

I modeled Martin Thompson Funeral Home as closely to THC as possible. That meant: a full-time funeral director, an apprentice, front-desk staff answering calls from 9 a.m. to 9 p.m., seven days a week, and impeccable service and a polished, professional atmosphere.

The problem? Advertising money. The remodel had gutted my budget. I had exactly zero dollars for billboards, newspaper ads, or any kind of traditional marketing. So, I became the advertising.

Enter my "book." I called it *Everything You Ever Wanted to Know About Funeral Service but Were Afraid to Ask*. In reality, it wasn't a book at all. It was a glorified spiral-bound binder from Kinko's.

Inside, I tore apart corporate funeral homes, exposing their pricing tricks, upsells, and questionable practices. If *The American Way of Death* was a best-seller exposing the corporate funeral industry, my binder was the local Texas edition, with a side of righteous indignation.

My strategy? Get in front of every pastor and church leader in the area. If I could meet one pastor a day, I figured word-of-mouth would spread. Problem was, I launched this grand plan in December, the busiest time of year for churches. Most pastors were knee-deep in nativity scenes, choir rehearsals, and Christmas Eve services.

I met a few, but let's just say that most of them weren't exactly dying to talk about funerals during the holiday season.

But in early January, a man in a suit showed up at the door.

"I'm with the Texas Funeral Service Commission. Here for your inspection."

Finally.

Thirty minutes later, he handed me a single sheet of paper—almost as spectacular as when I received my funeral director's license.

"You're open."

Just like that, Martin Thompson Funeral Home was officially open for business.

Only problem? No one knew it.

That night, the phone rang. It was one of the pastors I had visited.

"Mr. Thompson, we've had a death in our congregation. I'm at the family home right now and wanted to see if you were open yet."

I made the call that night, met with the family the next day, and three days later, we conducted our first funeral.

Sometimes, you get little reminders that God has a plan.

Ten days later, another call from another pastor. Then, ten days after that, another.

One funeral every ten days wasn't exactly a fast-track to success, but at least we had a foot in the door. The gamble had officially begun.

40

FROM UNKNOWN TO UNSTOPPABLE: CONQUERING GRAPEVINE

When I opened Martin Thompson Funeral Home, I wanted it to be the THC of Grapevine—from the service to the ambiance, from the staffing to the pricing. Every detail had to be top-notch.

But there was one tiny problem: volume.

At THC, Dad had five hundred calls a year, which justified a large, full-time staff. At forty to fifty calls? Not so much. So, I had to get smart.

One of Dad's oldest friends, Kent Adair, a retired funeral director who had owned a successful funeral home in California, started volunteering his time at MTFH. Without Kent, I honestly don't know where I'd be.

We took a hard look at operations and quickly found obvious cuts:

+ 5 p.m. – 9 p.m. shift? Pointless if we had no calls. Gone.

+ Sunday staffing? Not needed unless we had services. Cut.

+ Saturdays? Half-day if we weren't busy.

+ Apprentice position? Unnecessary when I was already working from 7 a.m. until late every day—for free.

By trimming overhead, we kept service quality high while ensuring the business stayed financially healthy.

One summer, after handling a funeral for a well-known local lady, I decided to attend the monthly Chamber of Commerce meeting. I walked in alone, found a table, and sat down—completely unnoticed. Then, I heard a voice: "I didn't know you were a Chamber member."

I turned to see Edie Gillette, a powerhouse of a woman who seemed to know everyone in town.

"I've actually been to every luncheon since I joined," I told her.

She shook her head and smirked. "Coming to a monthly luncheon isn't being a Chamber member. You have to get involved."

And just like that, Edie took me under her wing. She signed me up as a Chamber Ambassador, the group that welcomed every new business to town. Ribbon cuttings were happening constantly—and I was at every single one. It didn't take long before people started recognizing my name.

Then Edie pulled me into Rotary, where I met Phil Cloud, a man with the best nickname in town (before it was synonymous with someone else): Puff Daddy. Phil introduced me to Ambucs, a civic club dedicated to giving back to the community. It was full of guys like me—fun-loving, hardworking, and passionate about making a difference.

Suddenly, I wasn't just *in* Grapevine. I was a part of Grapevine.

Between Rotary luncheons on Tuesdays, Ambuc luncheons on Thursdays, Chamber luncheons on Fridays, and committee luncheons on other weekdays, I never had to buy lunch again.

More importantly? The phone started ringing.

People don't pick a funeral home because of a billboard or an ad. They pick one because they trust you. By showing up at every luncheon, ribbon cutting, committee meeting, and charity event, I became the funeral director people knew and trusted.

At the time, Grapevine's two longtime funeral homes—Foust and Lucas—had both been swallowed up by large corporations. The problem with corporate ownership? There was no full-time funeral director on staff; no presence in the Chamber, Rotary, or Ambucs; no community connection; and no local church involvement. What's more, they were out of touch, overpriced, and impersonal.

And that's how I won.

By cutting costs, lowering prices, and embedding myself in the community, Martin Thompson Funeral Home didn't just compete. We dominated. It didn't take long before over 80 percent of the business in Grapevine came through my doors.

And to think—I started this journey knowing no one in town. Now I was Grapevine's go-to funeral home.

And the best part?

I was just getting started.

41

FROM JOINER TO COUNTRY UNDERTAKER

My dad always prided himself on not being a "joiner." Sure, he was a member of the Knights of Columbus and paid dues to the Sierra Club, but he never saw the point in networking through chambers, Rotary, or civic clubs. Dad worked. Period.

But times had changed. And if I wanted Martin Thompson Funeral Home to thrive in Grapevine, I knew that sitting behind my desk and waiting for calls wouldn't cut it. I had to get out there.

The Grapevine Chamber of Commerce had a mission: Collaborate. Communicate. Connect. Advocate. For me, the Chamber was a goldmine. It introduced me to great friends. It connected me with business owners who could help grow MTFH. And it gave me a platform to promote my business without spending a dime on advertising.

What started as a casual lunch quickly turned into committee assignments. Before I knew it, I wasn't just attending meetings—I was leading them. I became a Chamber Ambassador, then a board member, and ultimately Chairman of the Board of the Grapevine Chamber of Commerce.

This put me right in the middle of major developments like:

+ The opening of the Gaylord Texan
+ The launch of Cowboys Golf Club
+ The rise of Grapevine Mills Mall
+ Several major hotel developments

It was an exciting time—not just for me, but for Grapevine itself.

On par with the Chamber of Commerce, The Rotary Club's mission is all about service, integrity, and global goodwill—but let's be honest, it was also where Grapevine's top business minds gathered. These were the polished folks who held positions as attorneys, bankers, doctors, ministers, and small business owners. And let's not forget, the food was always good.

If Rotary was about polish, then Ambucs was about grit. Their mission? Providing mobility and independence for people with disabilities. And let me tell you—this was my kind of group. I met some of my closest lifelong friends here:

Phil "Puff Daddy" Cloud – A banker whose family had deep Grapevine roots. His bank supported everything in town, and his last name earned him the nickname *Puff*. I threw in *Daddy* because, well, that was a thing back then. He put up with it.

Ron Stacy – His family was famous for their "Burning Your Money" furniture commercials. Ron ran his brother's new Grapevine furniture store and was one of the biggest supporters of Grapevine—and of me.

Mark Stanfield – If you wanted to meet a guy whose *polish was his heart*, it was Mark. Hugely successful, but the kind of guy who shared everything he had with those in need.

Ronny Nordling – Another banker, but more importantly, a Grapevine insider who knew everyone and everything going on in town.

The Parkers – Owners of Willhoite's, a legendary Grapevine restaurant-by-day, full-blown bar-by-night spot. These guys knew how to mix business, community, and a good time.

And it didn't stop there—Ambucs had City Council members, CVB executives, and other movers and shakers.

Before long, my involvement in Ambucs led to something else...

Most of the guys in Ambucs played golf, and they loved tournaments. It started with invites to charity golf tournaments, but soon, they pulled me into their regular Sunday morning tee time—the first slot of the day.

We teed off just as the sun cracked the horizon. That meant if I wasn't already in Grapevine on a Saturday night, I had to wake up at 4:30 a.m. just to make it. But it was worth it.

These guys became my friends for life, adopting a "Fort Worth guy" and making him a "Grapevine guy." And, more than anything, they promoted my business.

One of our greatest projects was the Amtryke program—providing adaptive bicycles and tricycles for kids with mobility issues. These weren't just bikes. They gave kids who had never walked or ridden the chance to join their siblings on rides. I can't count how many times I saw a child's face light up with joy when they finally got to ride. And the impact was far greater than just fun—families reported kids showing improvement in walking, communication, and confidence after using the bikes.

The year I was Ambucs president, we attended our national meeting in Memphis, where we launched bikes for injured veterans, giving them the chance to ride again with their kids. Our club gave away about one hundred bikes and trikes a year—one of the highest totals in the country.

I've had a lot of proud moments in my career, but being an Ambuc ranks right at the top.

—◦—

Once I had become a full-blown joiner, I expanded beyond Grapevine to the Chambers in Southlake Chamber, Colleyville, Mid-Cities, and Northeast.

One day, Kent Adair—my friend, mentor, and longtime funeral director—looked at me and said, "Martin, if you're not careful, you're going to become a country undertaker."

I laughed. "Kent, if I don't become a country undertaker, I'm gonna go broke."

And that's exactly what I became. Not just a funeral director—but Grapevine's funeral director.

I wasn't just in the community. I was part of it. And that made all the difference.

42

CANDICE:
THE WORLDLY ONE

So far, I've written extensively about my son, Jon, and other family members, but only briefly about my daughter, Candice. The truth is, our relationship has had its ups and downs—and if I could go back, I'd do some things differently. Still, Candice has lived an extraordinary story, and it belongs right here alongside the rest of the families'.

In 2001, Martin Thompson Funeral Home in Grapevine was starting to find its stride. Life felt busy but steady.

Then came a phone call that changed everything.

I was driving back from a graveside service in Wichita Falls when Candice called. She had just moved to New York with a friend after graduating from my alma mater, Texas Wesleyan (yes, she followed me to "Teeny Weeny"). She loved Spanish so much that she made it her major, and she truly immersed herself in it. She'd spent two semesters in Cuernavaca, Mexico, at Monterrey University, polishing her Spanish far beyond Tex-Mex version. Then she spent her final semester in Barcelona, where she immersed herself in Castilian Spanish. By graduation, North Richland Hills, Texas, just wasn't enough for her. She needed the world.

That summer, she and her friend packed their belongings into a shared moving van and headed east, planning to find an apartment once they arrived in New York. On September 10, Candice called to say they'd finally found one: a one-room apartment on Madison Avenue for $2,700 a month. (Yes, you read that right.)

The landlord wanted me to cosign the lease. My first response was: "Candice, you don't even have a job!"

She assured me she had an interview the next morning with Merrill Lynch, which was in Building 7 of the World Trade Center. We haggled, argued, and finally landed on a compromise: if she got the job and her friend's parents cosigned half, I'd do it.

The next morning, I was in the shower when Janice came running in. "I think you'd better come see this."

I dried off and walked into the kitchen, where *Good Morning America* was showing smoke pouring from a gaping hole in the World Trade Center. They were speculating about what happened. I tried to call Candice. Nothing. For what felt like an eternity, the phones were dead.

And then, finally, it rang.

Candice hadn't left for her interview yet. She had already called the woman she was supposed to meet, who told her to reschedule that afternoon. As we were talking, the second plane hit.

This wasn't an accident. This was a terrorist attack.

I begged her to come home, but she insisted she was okay, staying with friends in Midtown, and would check back with Merrill Lynch later. But by the end of the day, Building 7 collapsed along with Towers 1 and 2. The interview would never take place. Merrill Lynch, like so many companies, was scattered, displaced, and forever changed.

Candice never got that interview.

Instead, she stayed. Stubborn, determined—maybe a little of both—she made her way in New York, taking a job at a bar called Faces and Names in the theater district. Officially, she worked until 4 a.m., but in true New York fashion, the bar didn't close until the last customer left, which meant Candice often worked until sunrise.

A couple years later, Candice moved to Washington, DC and eventually landed a great job that later brought her back home.

Looking back, I see things more clearly. When Eleanor and I divorced, Jon came to live with me, while Candice remained close to her mother. My bond with Jon was strong, and Candice's bond with her mom was equally strong. Life and circumstances simply pulled us in different directions.

And so today, we don't have the relationship I would like. But if there's one thing I've learned in my life, it's that people and relationships have a way of circling back. In my heart, I hope Candice and I find that path.

The week after 9/11 was strange in Grapevine. My funeral home sat at the end of the runway at DFW International Airport, and suddenly, with all flights grounded, the skies were silent. I hadn't realized how constant the low rumble of airplanes had become—but when it was gone, the silence felt deafening.

Everywhere you went, gas stations, restaurants—you'd see stranded travelers. Hundreds of people were stuck in town, desperate to rent cars or rides home. Some had very little money, and many of us locals did what we could—buying meals, sharing rides, anything to help our unexpected guests.

If that was what we were experiencing in Grapevine, I can only imagine what Candice was experiencing in New York. Not only had her dreams of starting a new career been ripped away, but she and her friends went down to the site itself to volunteer, to see with their own eyes what had happened. She later confided in me that it had shaken her deeply. And I believe it changed her— just as it changed all of us. It was a moment that altered lives, redirected paths, and left scars we'll always carry. And I pray we'll never see another day like that again.

43

DOCKING DILEMMAS

When I married Janice, I moved into her charming cottage-style home in the TCU area. Janice loved her home—every quirky inch of it. From the hundred-year-old pecan tree in the front yard (probably one of the biggest in Fort Worth) to the equally ancient walnut tree in the backyard, her house had more character and charm than a whole season of HGTV home makeover shows.

The one thing she didn't love? The idea of moving to Grapevine.

We'd discussed it more times than I care to admit, but it was always a hard no. Looking back, I'm glad we stayed put. But staying in Fort Worth meant I had to commute to Grapevine every day—a trek that felt like an endurance challenge from *American Ninja Warrior*. Every road between the two cities was under construction, which meant lanes were closed and detours led to more detours. It was an hour drive on a good day, two on a bad one.

After a few months of this daily traffic purgatory, I realized I needed a backup plan.

Back when I renovated the Dorris House, I had big plans for the third floor—my personal office and a bedroom for those nights when I just couldn't face the drive home. Which was fine until the fire marshal showed up.

"You can't use the third floor of a commercial building for residential space unless it has a separate fire escape," he told me.

That was news to me. But this particular fire marshal was also a Grapevine Ambuc, and after a slight pause, he gave me a knowing wink and said, "Just call it storage."

Who was I to argue?

So, the third floor became my "storage" space. I equipped it with a desk and chairs—perfect for storing work essentials; a bed and dresser—great for organizing old clothes, of course; and paintings on the walls—because, well, you gotta store artwork somewhere. Everything was very neatly arranged. I take my storage solutions seriously.

Later, when I moved the funeral home behind the hospital, I lucked out—the building came with a nightman's apartment, doubling as my office and a place to crash when needed.

But when I moved again—this time to the Main Street funeral home, the oldest in town—the second-floor restrooms had long been removed. And with road construction still turning my daily commute into a slow-motion car chase, I needed another plan.

Enter my brilliant idea: a Carver Aft Cabin cruiser.

I bought the boat from a guy on Lake Texoma and had it moved to a marina on Lake Grapevine, and just like that, I had a new home away from home.

My boat, affectionately named "Diggit," had all the comforts of home and then some: two bedrooms, a kitchen with a dining area, a spacious salon with a couch and big-screen TV, and a back deck for morning coffee and evening drinks. I had never slept better in my life.

You know that old saying: "The two happiest days in a boat owner's life are the day he buys it and the day he sells it?" Not me. I loved that boat

Living on the boat was the easy part.

The hard part was docking it.

Diggit had two big engines, so steering was mostly done with the engines, especially when leaving and (more importantly) returning to the dock. Some days, I nailed it like a seasoned captain. Other days? Not so much. The regulars at the marina quickly learned that my docking could be an event, and they never missed a show.

"Oh boy, here comes Martin—grab a beer, this should be good!"

But Jon, my son, was a natural. Maybe it was all those video games—he could maneuver that boat like he was playing Grand Theft Auto: Marina Edition. He made it look effortless, while I made it look like a slow-motion car wreck on water.

One day, my dear friend Steve Stinson, who was battling stage-four cancer, called and asked if I knew anyone selling a boat like mine. Steve and his wife Nikki had always dreamed of retiring on a lake, but with his health, they knew that day might not come.

At first, I told him I didn't know of anyone selling. Then it hit me. *Everything is for sale if you think about it.*

Steve was one of the toughest guys I knew, and he was battling the cancer with grit and humor. At our Ambuc meetings, we had a sergeant-at-arms who would fine members for everything from making the news to doing something dumb in public or wearing something ridiculous. One day, he asked Steve to stand up in the middle of lunch.

"I've seen a lot, but I have NEVER seen this. You, my friend, are wearing a fanny pack."

Steve didn't miss a beat. He pointed at the bag strapped to his waist and said, "You mean my chemo pump?"

The sergeant-at-arms immediately fined himself.

That was Steve.

He even played golf with that chemo pump on, and still he hit a pitching wedge 160 yards and drove the ball 300 yards over the corner on Hole 5 at Mockingbird.

A fanny pack? Please.

That night, Steve and Nikki came out for a sunset cruise and fell in love with the boat. The next night, they brought Steve's mom for another ride.

When Steve asked, "How much do you want for it?" I quoted a price I didn't think he'd take.

Before I could blink, his mom pulled out a check and handed it to me. And just like that, I had sold my beloved boat.

As bittersweet as it was, I knew it was the right thing to do.

Steve told me many times that after his brutal chemo treatments, being on that boat was the only thing keeping him going.

For his last year, he and Nikki lived his dream—on the water.

CHAPEL CHARADES:
FROM DREAM TO DOLLHOUSE
TO DESPERATION

Year after year, Martin Thompson Funeral Home kept growing, and the Dorris House, as charming and historic as it was, was starting to feel like a shoebox. Every available space was being used, the small carriage house in the back doubled as a chapel, and some visitations were crammed into areas never meant to hold people. It was clear: I needed a real chapel.

I decided to expand by building a new, larger chapel on the side of the house. To make sure it fit the historic aesthetic and matched the architecture of the Dorris House, I hired an architect who specialized in preserving Tarrant County's oldest buildings. This ensured it would blend seamlessly into the neighborhood and give us a proper space for services.

Since we were in Grapevine's historic district, I had to get approval from the Historic Commission before taking it to the City Council. No problem, right?

At the first meeting, the Historic Commission seemed pleased with the design.

"Looks great!"

"This will complement the house beautifully!"

"Come back next month with more detailed drawings."

Feeling confident, I gave my architect the green light for full plans.

On the day of the second presentation, I had the chance to play a very exclusive golf course. So my dilemma was: Play golf or fight a historic commission? *Golf, obviously.*

I finished most of my round but left a couple holes early to make it to the meeting *just* in time, strolling in as my architect wrapped up his presentation.

Heads were nodding again—always a good sign. Then came the questions.

First Historic Member: "You know, the Dorris House is one of our most historic homes in Grapevine. I think the chapel should be shorter, not taller, than the house."

Okay, fine. We can lower the roofline a bit.

Second Historic Member: "And it shouldn't come all the way to the front of the Dorris House. Take it back a few feet."

Sure, we can move it back a little.

Third Historic Member: "I'd like it to be narrower, not so wide."

Now we're getting a little cramped, but okay . . .

Fourth Historic Member: "I don't think it should be connected to the Dorris House at all."

Wait . . . what?

Suddenly, my grand chapel was starting to look like a Victorian dollhouse—shorter, thinner, and squeezed into an awkward little spot.

I spoke up. "I really need a proper chapel, not a dollhouse."

That's when one of them dropped the bombshell.

"Why not just tear down the carriage house and put the chapel there?"

That wasn't remotely what I wanted.

Since no progress was being made, I took the entire committee—yes, the whole bunch of them—and my architect to Dallas to look at the carriage houses behind historic homes on Ross Ave, thinking that seeing real-life examples would help. Maybe they'd finally understand what I was going for. Maybe—just maybe—they'd give me a solid answer.

They did.

They drew me a crude elevation of what they thought would look good, which was essentially a wooden, rustic barn. Did they forget this was a funeral home, not a ranch?

At this point, I had spent a great deal of money and even more time, and I was right back where I started.

I knew what I had to do.

I had to move, but where?

45

KELLER'S REJECTION, MANSFIELD'S ACCEPTANCE, AND THE DISASTER IN BETWEEN

At this point in my career, I had gotten deeply involved with the Texas Funeral Directors Association and found myself on the convention committee for the upcoming event in Fort Worth.

Meetings? Check.

Golf? Absolutely.

Ending the day at the hotel bar like every good funeral convention? Of course.

One evening, during one of these bar-side chats, a guy I knew from my brother's funeral business days pulled up a stool next to me. His family had been in the funeral business too, but they had sold out to SCI in the '80s. He was now working for SCI, but itching to get back into independent ownership. That's when he hit me with the opportunity of a lifetime.

"I have a shot at buying some of SCI's free-standing funeral homes in Fort Worth," he said. "You need more space, right? One of them is in Grapevine."

My chapel expansion plans had just gone up in smoke. I needed a bigger place. And this guy had a plan. It seemed like the perfect fit: an easy expansion with smooth sailing ahead.

Little did I know, I was about to board the *Titanic*.

First up on the list was a church in Keller that we planned to turn into a funeral home—but there was a catch. Keller had an ordinance requiring a Specific Use Permit for any new funeral home. So, we drew up our plans, took them to the city council, and presented our case.

BAM! DENIED.

One council member looked me dead in the eye and said, "A funeral home doesn't fit the vibe of an old Texas town."

Are you kidding me?!

Doesn't fit the vibe?!

Have you ever seen an old Western? The Undertaker was always one of the first buildings in town! They had coffins ready before the first shootout! And *now*, a funeral home is out of place?!

I was shocked, but not defeated.

We had the option to appeal, but it would take ninety days.

Instead of sitting around, I decided to take action.

I went door to door and introduced myself to every business owner in Old Town Keller. I explained our vision and handed out glowing letters of recommendation, then I joined their chamber and got involved. I even pulled out a letter of support from Mayor William D. Tate of Grapevine—the same mayor who initially didn't think Grapevine needed another funeral home but later became a supporter.

On the night of the appeal, I stepped up and told the city council a simple story:

"Keller wants to be a great city. You want schools, doctors, libraries, restaurants, businesses . . . everything that makes a town great. But when it's time to celebrate a life well lived, when a family is grieving, they have to go somewhere else."

That night, we became the first funeral home in Keller—

which proves that persistence pays off, a handshake means something, and old Texas charm still wins.

While the Keller saga played out, I was also negotiating with the owners of a very old funeral home in Mansfield. Talks were smooth. The deal was sealed. And suddenly, I had a busy, beautiful funeral home in Mansfield. Everything was falling into place . . . until I opened the *Star-Telegram* one morning and read this on the front page:

"Martin Thompson buys historic funeral home in Fort Worth, longtime competitor of his father's business."

Wait . . . WHAT?

I never bought a funeral home in Fort Worth.

I called my so-called partner. "What the hell is this?"

That's when he dropped the bombshell: he had purchased the funeral home down the street from my dad—and he had used MY NAME to do it and never told me.

My dad had been my rock. He had supported me every step of the way. Now, it looked like I had stabbed him in the back.

And if that wasn't bad enough, money started disappearing. A *lot* of money. It was suddenly missing, mismanaged, or misused with no explanations. So I hired an attorney—which meant mediation, arbitration, and more headaches than I could count. Ultimately, I realized something devastating: there was not only no winning this battle, there was no way to fix the mess. The only option? Get out.

With no other choice, I had to sell everything. Everything I had worked for, built, and fought for . . . GONE.

For the second time, I found myself starting over. But if you know anything about Martin Thompson, you know one thing . . .

I wasn't staying down for long.

46

A PROFITABLE PARTNERSHIP
AND A PRICEY PROBLEM

After the disaster of my last business venture, I knew I couldn't just pack it in and call it a day. My family was counting on me—my wife, my son, and his family. Failure was not an option.

Fortunately, in the fire sale of my previous business, I managed to keep one golden egg: *no non-compete clause*. That gave me no restrictions, no legal handcuffs, and no boundaries. I could start over anywhere I wanted. And where did I want to be? *Grapevine.*

As luck would have it, I had struck up a friendship with the president of the western division of Stewart Enterprises. Stewart owned Foust Funeral Home, the oldest in Grapevine, housed in yet another historic home on Main Street. But the place was handling less than a hundred calls a year—barely enough to keep the lights on. It was a forgotten relic, run more out of obligation than passion, and Stewart didn't know what to do with it.

So, I did what I do best: I pitched a plan.

I headed to Dallas to meet with the big bosses—the president and his regional VP—and laid it all out.

1) I'd take over Foust Funeral Home as the manager;
2) I'd work for the bare minimum of a funeral home manager's salary; and
3) instead of a fat paycheck, I wanted a cut of the gross profits.

They looked at me like I had two heads. Then, skeptical but curious, they said, "You realize this place isn't making any gross profits, right?"

I responded by reiterating that I had zero risk for them, that if I failed, they lost nothing, and that if I succeeded, they turned a profit.

After some back and forth, they agreed to let me run the funeral home my way—I just couldn't stray too far from Stewart's playbook.

I had my shot.

On Monday morning, Jon and I stepped into a time capsule. Foust was a beautiful colonial mansion from the late 1800s—but it was neglected, worn down, and felt stale and lifeless.

I was back in the game, though, just like when I first opened Martin Thompson Funeral Home—only nobody knew it yet.

So, I did what any self-respecting funeral director would do: I hit the streets. I called on every pastor I knew. I shouted about Foust at chamber meetings, Ambuc meetings, Rotary meetings—anywhere people would listen.

Foust Funeral Home was right in the middle of downtown Grapevine. The location was perfect, especially since Grapevine was the festival capital of Texas. It held the Main Street Festival in the spring and Grapefest in the fall, homecoming parades, and even something called Butterfly Flutterbye (still not sure what that was). We were smack dab in the middle of all the action.

So, I started walking to meetings. I set up booths at all the festivals. And Halloween? We decked out the front and handed out candy to the kids.

I was in my element, and I was loving every second of it.

At some point, Stewart gave me a budget to spruce up the place—and I used it wisely. I took every dime out of the gross profits, and bit by bit, word spread. By the end of year one, I had more than doubled the calls, and we turned a profit for the first time in years. In the subsequent three years, the funeral home continued to grow, profits soared, and Foust was making money hand over fist.

That's when corporate noticed—and Stewart had a problem.

A little funeral home manager in Grapevine was making more money than some of their senior vice presidents. Suddenly, I was on their radar. The whispers started. The jealousy crept in. New Orleans HQ started asking questions.

And then, one day, my senior VP walked into my office and never left.

To his credit, he was open to brainstorming ideas. We collaborated on strategies and tried to figure out how Stewart could do better—for both the company and the families we served.

But then came The Big Shakeup.

My biggest ally—the president of the western division—got promoted to sales, which meant he left funeral operations behind. Luckily, my regional manager, now a great friend, fought for me tooth and nail.

"Yes, he's making a lot of money," he argued, "but Stewart is making even more because of him!"

But corporate didn't care.

One by one, my allies were eliminated.

Then, the inevitable happened.

Stewart sat me down. "Martin, we can't honor this agreement anymore."

Translation: You're making too much money, and we don't like it.

Suddenly, the friendly vibe was gone. Bad blood started brewing. The lower managers got nasty. I knew my time was up.

I had given thirty-six years of my life to this business—my blood, sweat, and tears were in it. I had not only built something real, I had turned a dying business into a thriving one. And now, I was being pushed out.

I wasn't about to take a step backward.

It was time to start over. Again.

47

BACK TO BASICS:
FORT WORTH OR BUST

t was 2012, and you'd think I'd seen it all. I had learned from one of the best—my dad. I'd built my own funeral home. I had partnered up, gotten burned, and bounced back. I'd even dabbled in the corporate world and made them more money than they knew what to do with.

But if I'd learned anything, it was this: Just when you think you've got it all figured out, life throws you a curveball. Or, in my case: A casket on wheels.

After all the ups and downs, it was time to return to my roots. Fort Worth was calling me back. And this time, I was doing things my way.

I founded Martin Thompson & Son Funeral Home with a simple goal: Blend old-school service with new-school value.

The industry was changing. Cremation was now over half the business, and many traditional funeral homes resisted the change —and were losing business because of it. The ones that embraced cremation? They were gouging families, charging insane prices for simple services. Then there were the pop-up discount funeral homes, operating out of warehouses or even without a real facility at all. Sure, they were cheap, but service levels were nonexistent.

It was in this climate that I saw the opportunity to offer affordable, meaningful services, keep pricing lean and transparent, and deliver first-class service, no matter what.

So, I set out to find the ideal location.

I found a modest, well-kept building on the south side of Fort Worth. If you squinted hard enough, and had a little imagination, it was perfect.

Since I had no idea how this venture would be received, my family pitched in. Jon went to work at Thompson's Harveson & Cole to help out while I became a one-man band. Literally.

I made calls.

I took calls.

I met with families.

I planned funerals.

I handled paperwork—death certificates, guest books, service folders, prayer cards.

I was the janitor and the yardman.

And the schedule?

On call Sunday through Saturday. Working from open to close. Attending every visitation.

You get the picture.

This time around, I didn't just seek out pastors. I made a big push to connect with hospice groups. I knocked on every door that would open and told anyone who would listen what we were doing.

And it worked.

I kept our prices lean, our service top-notch, and I made sure families felt cared for—the way my dad always taught me. Sure, I found time for a little golf, but let's be honest . . .

That's where the best networking happens, right?

Before long, my little brand of funeral service started gaining traction. Within a year, I brought Jon on full-time. A year after that, we added two more employees. Then two more. By 2020, my one-man show had grown to five hundred calls a year.

From scratch.
In a changing industry.
In a market flooded with competition.
But this time, I wasn't just starting over.
This time, it felt like a well-earned victory lap.

48

FROM TYPEWRITERS TO TECH TITANS

By 2012, running a funeral home was a completely different ball game than when I started in 1976. And by different, I mean it was like comparing a rotary phone to the latest iPhone.

Back in '76, everything was manual. Death certificates, prayer cards, guest books—all typed out, one key at a time. If you were lucky, you had one of those electric typewriters with the little golf-ball typing element you could swap out for different fonts. That was our version of cutting-edge tech.

My Aunt Bernadine was the fastest typist I'd ever seen. She hand-typed every guest book and prayer card for Catholic funerals, sometimes cranking out hundreds in a single event. She typed every letter, every document, and even some of my school term papers. Looking back, she was basically our first "computer."

By 1980, my brother Vic and I finally convinced Dad to buy a real computer. Just like that, THC leapt from ancient civilization to modern technology. Dad didn't think much of it, but to us, it felt like going from a mule to a Cadillac overnight.

When I opened Martin Thompson Funeral Home in 1998, I decided to do things differently. We were fully computerized from the very beginning. No bulk casket buying. No hand-typed service folders. Everything was printed in-house, clean and professional. I even jumped into advertising with both feet. If there was a place to put our name, I was there—multiple newspapers, church bulletins, school directories, sports calendars. And yes, six different Yellow Pages. Families could find me alphabetically, no matter which book they picked up.

One of my favorite projects was a TV commercial where I walked through the funeral home explaining our services. At the end, I tipped my pure beaver black cowboy hat and said, "Walk on, Sue," as our black Percheron draft horse pulled a hearse off-screen. That one spot got more comments than anything else I've done in fifty years.

I had signed a contract to air the commercial on CNN and a few other cable channels. Because my budget wasn't huge, most of the ads ran at unscheduled times—midnight, two in the morning, odd hours when you'd assume nobody was watching.

Well, that was about the time President George W. Bush decided Saddam Hussein's time had run its course, and the US launched the invasion of Iraq. CNN had crews on hotel rooftops in Baghdad broadcasting around the clock, and even Baghdad Bob was on TV denying our presence while CNN showed footage of American tanks just a few blocks away.

With America—and Grapevine—glued to their televisions at all hours, my little commercial started popping up in between war updates. Suddenly, my midnight slots were prime time.

A few days later, I was walking through a grocery store in Grapevine when a little boy tugged at his mom and said, "That's the Walk on Sue guy!"

I may not have been Tom Brokaw, but for a moment, I was a cable news star.

By 2012, though, the ground had shifted. The Yellow Pages became extinct. Professionally built ones replaced homemade websites. Families weren't circling ads in the newspaper any-more—they were Googling funeral homes, and Google Ads had become the number one way to be found. Bidding for placement meant the highest bidder got the family's call. SEO was suddenly as important as embalming fluid.

Of course, learning to play in Google's sandbox came with its own set of headaches. The deal with Google Ads is simple: you set a daily budget and assign a dollar amount for each time someone clicks on your ad. At first, I thought I had figured it out. I set my budget, got my clicks, and waited for the phone to ring.

However, I then started noticing something strange. By noon each day, my budget was gone. I had been "clicked out." So, I did what any stubborn funeral director would do: I kept increasing the budget, and then I increased it again, and then I increased it again. Still, every day, by lunchtime, the money was gone.

Finally, I hired someone who understood all the things I still don't. He delved into the data, tracked the IP addresses, and iden-tified the issue. There weren't dozens of families searching for funeral services. It was *one single IP address,* clicking my ad a couple of hundred times every morning.

Turns out, that's one way to beat the competition. Not exactly the kind of professional courtesy Dad had taught me about back in the Yellow Pages days. These days, the competition isn't always across the street—sometimes it's hiding behind a keyboard.

Even the casket world was changing. In the '80s and '90s, for-eign-made caskets were considered cheap and unreliable. But by 2012, the quality had caught up. A guy in Dallas was importing thousands of Chinese and Mexican caskets, delivering them within twenty-four hours, just like US-made ones, but at thirty cents on the dollar. At first, I hesitated. Buy foreign caskets? But in the end, my priority has always been service and value. If I could save a family money without sacrificing quality, that's what mattered.

Fast-forward to 2024, and marketing looks nothing like when I started. We use drones for property videos. We run Facebook and YouTube campaigns. We hire specialists for SEO, Google Ads, and social media. Families can plan a funeral or cremation from their couch—filling out forms, making service selections, even getting interactive price estimates without ever leaving home.

One of the biggest game changers has been companies like FDLIC. They've transformed how we market, manage websites, and even handle financing. What used to take hours of paperwork can now be done in minutes online.

Back in 1976, we wouldn't have believed any of this was possible.

And if the past is any indicator . . . who knows what's coming next?

49

FUNERAL MOVES & APRIL FOOLS

I n March 2020, I got a call from my sister that felt like the setup for the world's weirdest prank.

"Cook Children's Hospital wants to buy the 8th Ave property."

The offer was too good to resist, but here was the catch: the closing date was April 1st—April Fool's Day. And the time frame to move out? Thirty days.

Jon and I both knew we wanted to keep the Thompson's Harveson & Cole name alive, but we had no idea where we'd go next. And if that wasn't enough, Covid was just starting to rear its ugly head. So now, in addition to moving a funeral home, we had a pandemic to contend with. Perfect timing.

This was the first time I had really spent much time at THC since walking out the door in 1998, so walking through those old halls was like stepping into a time capsule. The furniture was exactly where it was the day I left, the pictures were hung in the same spots, and the casket selection room was just as I remembered it.

At first, I was there to take inventory and see what needed moving. But as the days passed, I found myself drowning in memories. Every room . . . every painting . . . every chair, table, and couch carried stories—stories of my dad, my brother, my grandparents, my aunts, and the many friends and colleagues who had worked there over the years.

I made sure no one caught me, but I was grieving—not just for what had been, but for what could have been. It was bittersweet, to say the least.

Then came the hard part—finding a new place, moving seventy years' worth of history, and getting licensed in thirty days.

No pressure, right?

But like always, God had a plan.

A few years earlier, I'd looked at a church that had closed. At the time, I thought it was too big for what I needed. But now? It was a menu of perfect checkmarks:

A magnificent chapel.

Great parking.

Plenty of land.

Solid structure.

I called Grace Presbytery in Dallas, who owned the church. She asked me when I wanted to come look at the property.

"Look at it?" I said. "No, no. I don't want to look at it. I want to know when I can GET it."

Turns out, Ridglea Presbyterian was using it temporarily while their own church was being remodeled, but they were moving out on April 30th.

That night, I had moving vans lined up in the parking lot.

As terrible as Covid was, it gave us one unexpected advantage—we could renovate without disrupting services. Because funerals were limited to ten people, many families postponed services altogether, so it was the perfect time to make the new space our own.

As I looked around at our new home, it hit me: I worked at

THC for twenty-two years, and I'd left to start my own funeral home for another twenty-two years. Now, I was back—this time in charge.

God thing? Absolutely.

April Fool's joke? Maybe just a little.

One thing's for sure—God's got a sense of humor.

50

RENOVATION ODYSSEY

When the opportunity to buy Thompson's Harveson & Cole came up, Jon and I hit the ground running to find the perfect location. We scoured S. Main, Camp Bowie, Magnolia St., Hulen, and the 7th St. district, but everything we found had the same problems—either too small, no parking, or requiring a fortune in renovations.

And guess who'd end up paying for that? Yep, the families.

That's when we circled back to John Knox Presbyterian Church. It had been sitting empty for five years, collecting dust, but when we really took a second look, we saw possibilities.

It had: 1) a massive stone-built chapel—beautiful, but in need of serious TLC; 2) an education building made of what we call "clinker brick"—or what others might call "drunken bricklayer style"; 3) a fellowship hall that had seen better days (maybe even better decades); and 4) a parking lot that hadn't been sealcoated since who-knows-when.

At first glance, it was a diamond in the rough—emphasis on *rough*. But I thought, *We can work with this.*

The first thing we tackled? The exterior.

We trimmed the trees (which had been staging a takeover). We put on a new roof and added gutters. We ripped out the old carport—goodbye, eyesore!—and replaced the rotted cedar shake siding with a stone veneer to match the chapel. We painted all the trim to give it a fresh look and added screens to the windows (because "ugly windows" weren't part of the plan). Last, we sealcoated the parking lot—goodbye, potholes!—moved the iron fence from 8th Ave, added flagpoles, pressure-washed the stone and brick, and transformed the overgrown courtyard into an artificial turf oasis with new fencing and a covered carport for our vehicles.

By the time we were done, the place looked brand new.

Then there was the chapel.

Walking in, you could tell it had potential, but it needed serious work. In short order: faded red carpet—gone. Yellowish laminate pews—outta here. Walls that hadn't been painted since Reagan? Time for a facelift.

We went all in and laid new dark walnut hardwood floors. We said goodbye to '70s grime with fresh paint on the walls and ceiling. We went elegant and timeless with custom pews made to match the new floors. We fixed the back wall (which had fabric covering broken speakers) and replaced it with textured sheetrock. We installed new lighting on the platform (altar) to create a warm, peaceful ambiance. And, finally, we uncovered the beautiful stained-glass windows, which had been hidden behind faded plexiglass for years, and my cousin, Shannon Reeves, and his son put in double-walled glass to showcase them properly.

When we were finished, the chapel space was twice the size of our 8th Ave location and ten times more beautiful.

Next, we moved on to the education wing and offices, which also got the revamp treatment: new flooring throughout, fresh paint to brighten up the space, and bathroom upgrades.

And that office furniture from 8th Ave? It looked even better in its new home.

Simple changes made for big impact.

But that fellowship hall—aka the biggest challenge?

The bathrooms made gas station restrooms look fancy. The drop ceiling, barely nine feet high, was not only missing panels, it had dingy lighting. I wouldn't have made a sandwich in the kitchen. And the walls were covered in dated, dark pine paneling.

Needless to say, we ripped everything out.

Once we removed the drop ceiling, we discovered twelve- to fifteen-foot ceilings that were *way* more impressive. The walls and ceiling got foam-insulation, then drywall, texture, and paint.

We added a second air conditioner (because Texas summers don't play) and painted the pine walls to make the room more inviting. The kitchen? Gutted and rebuilt with new catering equipment. We laid stunning tile flooring—even Janice was blown away—installed built-in speakers and large screens on each end for video tributes, and renamed it "The Drawing Room" to honor our 8th Ave location.

It was now a space I was proud to bring families into.

And none of this would have happened without an amazing team. Renovations sound simple on paper, but if not for Luis Prieto and his wife, Martha Cabrera, who worked tirelessly to bring the project to life, it would have remained an eyesore—or at least might have only been a step up from one. Their craftsmanship was unmatched, and they became lifelong friends along the way.

And thanks to Covid, we were able to complete everything without disrupting services.

Looking back, what started as a forgotten church turned into a beautiful, functional funeral home that would serve families for generations.

And once again, it was proof that sometimes, the best things happen when you least expect them.

51

FUNERAL SERVICE IN PANDEMIC TIMES

When I first started in the funeral business, dangerous diseases existed, but none that truly shook the industry—until the AIDS epidemic hit in the mid-1980s. Suddenly, we were confronted with something we didn't fully understand, and in those early years, there was real fear about how infectious it was, especially during embalming.

The first AIDS case at Thompson's Harveson & Cole was a moment of reckoning. Dad called me and my brother Vic into his office and said, "How can we ask our employees to do something we aren't willing to do ourselves?"

So, Vic and I made the call and did the embalming. Our protective equipment? Barely sufficient. Two pairs of gloves—each with a few too many holes. Two hospital gowns—thin and far from secure. No modern PPE—we improvised as best we could.

I remember that day vividly because I was wearing my favorite custom-made suit. At the end of the embalming, Vic glanced at my pants and asked, "What's that spot?"

I looked down, and my heart stopped. *Oh my God*, I thought, *that has to be the AIDS virus on my pants.*

Panic took over. That night, I drove home in nothing but a hospital gown after throwing my entire suit away in a biohazard bag.

I know now that that was an unnecessary response, but at the time, it felt warranted.

The AIDS epidemic was horrifying, particularly before we knew it couldn't be "caught" during embalming, but even it paled in comparison—at least in terms of sheer numbers—to Covid-19.

When Covid hit in early 2020, Fort Worth was slow to feel the full weight of it. We watched in disbelief as New York and other major cities were overwhelmed, but at first, it seemed distant—something happening *elsewhere*.

Then, the calls started coming in.

Families walked into my office, devastated, having spent weeks or months separated from their loved ones. They hadn't been there to hold their hand, to say goodbye, to offer comfort in their final moments. And now, even in death, they couldn't have a proper burial because the government forbade it.

I have been in funeral service nearly my entire life, and I've never seen grief like that. It wasn't just heart-wrenching—it was cruel.

By October 2020, Martin Thompson & Son and Thompson's Harveson & Cole were busier than ever, handling more Covid deaths than I care to remember.

One Sunday afternoon, I went out for a round of golf. Everything felt fine—until the last few holes, when my legs started aching. I thought, *That's odd, it's not even cart-path-only today.* Then, my back started hurting. By the time we finished, I felt awful.

I went straight home. Janice was in Brownwood at our farm, and by the next morning, I woke up feeling even worse. I searched online for Covid testing locations and found the earliest available appointment. When I arrived, the line of cars stretched for blocks—a two-and-a-half-hour wait for a drive-thru nose swab.

Finally, it was my turn. The nurse swabbed me, walked away, and returned a few minutes later. She leaned into my window. "You're positive."

As I sat in my car, the weight of those words hit me.

I had buried so many people who had died from Covid. *Was I next? Is this it? Am I going to make it a week? A month? Will I be in a hospital bed with masked nurses checking on me? Will I see my family again?*

I needed to think fast. I knew I couldn't go home—Janice's mom was living with us, and she was at high risk. So I grabbed my phone and booked a hotel room online, one where I could do everything digitally with no in-person contact. Then, I called Janice who immediately said she was coming home.

I told her I had already checked into a hotel so I wouldn't infect her and her mom. I asked her to pack a bag, leave it in the trunk of her car, and when she got home, I'd swing by, masked and gloved, to grab it.

I made it through, but so many didn't—including one of my best friends, Phil "Puff Daddy" Cloud. You'll recall that Phil was one of the first people to welcome me to Grapevine. He was my golf buddy, my Ambucs brother, and one of the best people I've ever known. We had played countless rounds together, worked on community projects, and laughed more times than I could count.

And then, in an instant—he was gone.

Even now, I miss him.

The funeral industry has weathered many storms, but nothing has changed it as drastically as Covid-19.

Funerals became virtual.

Viewings were limited to ten people.

Families grieved alone.

It was a painful time, but it also reminded me why I do this work. Even in a world turned upside down, people needed compassion, dignity, and someone to help carry the weight of loss.

And that's what we did.

Through AIDS, through Covid, through every challenge thrown our way—we adapted, persevered, and stood by the families who needed us most.

52

THE DREAM TEAM: A FUNERAL HOME'S BEST-KEPT SECRET

As I sit here today, reflecting on where we've been and where we're headed, I'm proud to say that our funeral homes aren't just growing—they're thriving.

Earlier last year, Jon had a bright idea: Why not throw our name in the ring for the *Star-Telegram's* DFW Favorites Award? It was formerly known as the Readers' Choice Award, and it provided an opportunity for families we've served, along with our friends and community, to vote for their favorite funeral home.

Well, wouldn't you know it?

Thompson's Harveson & Cole won Silver, and Martin Thompson & Son took home the Gold.

That's right—after 113 years in business, Thompson's Harveson & Cole finally got recognized. And Jon? He pulled it off in just twelve years, winning first place.

Well done, Son. This year, Thompson's Harveson & Cole secured Gold, and Martin Thompson & Son won Silver; maybe we'll keep flipping, who knows.

THE THC CREW

At Thompson's Harveson & Cole, I've been lucky enough to retain two of our best employees, Roger Kersten and Charles Surber—two men who represent the very best of funeral service.

Roger is a workhorse. The man never stops. He's been with us for nearly forty years, and families adore him. He wears more hats than a mannequin during a department store clearance sale. He's not only a master at meeting families and an expert in working funerals, he's the best cosmetologist I've ever seen (thanks to my dad's old-school training). If that wasn't enough, he's also a bird breeder with aviaries at TWO houses. I swear, Roger doesn't know the word "no." The funeral home wouldn't be the same without him.

Charles I've known since my Boy Scout days. He was an Eagle Scout from Troop 32 when I first joined, and by the time I got to Nolan, he was in his last year. Years later, I even bought furniture from his store before he closed up shop and joined us. Charles is a true gentleman—always impeccably dressed and a calming presence for grieving families. He carries himself with pride that's as rare as a hole-in-one. And because Charles lost his wife to Covid, he brings a deep level of compassion that only someone who's walked that road can truly understand. Like Roger, families love working with him.

And then there's **Martha**—my twin, or as we like to say, my *"Whommate."* Martha has always been in my corner, no matter what, and I can't thank anyone more than her for all she has done for me over the years. She is an incredible mother to what we affectionately call the "Mini Marthas"—Mary, Meagan, Molly, and Maddie. She poured herself into raising those girls, and it shows. Each one has grown into a successful, independent young woman who carries her mom's strength, humor, and heart.

It's amazing that Martha and I are not only twins, but we

probably share more similarities than is healthy. Same humor, same tastes, same favorite foods—we can't wait to show each other some silly Facebook post or video that only the two of us would find hilarious. Honestly, it's a little creepy how alike we are.

But what makes me proudest isn't just being her twin, it's hearing how she interacts with families and staff at the funeral home. She's steady, kind, and thoughtful, and has the same qualities that made her a wonderful mom. Having Martha by my side these days, both as a sister and as part of our team, is something I'll never take for granted.

Then there's **Sindee Sims,** a fellow 1976 graduate from Nolan High School. Sindee not only keeps our office running smoothly, she's also my dog Harveson's favorite person in the building—he greets her with more enthusiasm than he shows me. Outside the office, she's been a blessing to Janice and me, especially when it comes to caring for our dogs or helping with Janice's never-ending mission to feed every bird, squirrel, and stray cat within a five-mile radius. While I may have been burying animals as a six-year-old, Janice (with Sindee's help) is making sure they live fat and happy lives.

We also have **Lisa,** who brings warmth, charm, and a soothing voice to families calling in their time of need. Often, the first contact with a family is over the phone, and Lisa's kindness sets the tone for everything that follows.

And then, of course, **Luis Prieto** and his wife, **Martha Cabrera,** who hold down the fort at both THC and Martin Thompson & Son. I truly couldn't do this without them.

THE MTS CREW

Over at Martin Thompson & Son, I've passed the torch to Jon. I didn't just give him a name that people constantly misspell—I also handed him a thriving funeral home that continues to grow at a pace that even I didn't expect. To say I'm proud of Jon would be the understatement of the century. He is a phenomenal funeral director, an incredible husband to Brittany, and a devoted father to Palmer and Olivia (my two wonderful grandkids!).

Jon has grown MTS so much that a few years ago, we had to buy the building next door to expand our very cramped space. He and his top-notch team played a massive role in renovating it, and it turned out beautifully—bright, airy, and comfortable for both families and staff. Next up? Renovating the original building.

Luckily, Jon has his own Dream Team at MTS.

- **Peyton** is The Rockstar Embalmer. (I'm old enough that I shouldn't feel awkward saying this, but Peyton isn't just beautiful—she's also an incredibly talented embalmer.) She is one of the hardest-working people I know, dedicated to her craft and constantly learning more through embalming conferences. A true artist in restorative work, she brings families peace of mind during some of their most difficult moments.

- **David and Zach** are The Workhorses. These two are machines when it comes to meeting families, taking calls, and handling funerals. And they do it all without a single complaint.

- **Bessie and Jerald** are our Community Connectors. They've helped us serve families we might never have reached otherwise, expanding our ability to meet people where they are.

- **Sophia** is The Office Powerhouse. Always smiling, always working hard, and—thank goodness—fluent in Spanish. She helps countless families navigate the process in their native language. I've tried to learn Spanish myself, but let's just say it's not my strong suit.

+ **Gary** is The Best Crematory Operator in the Business. With cremation being a significant part of our profession, having the right person in charge of the crematory is essential—and Gary runs it with utmost professionalism. He keeps it what I call "Channel 5 Ready" (meaning if a news crew showed up, it would be spotless!).

And the best part? His son, **Jeff**, represents us well at night, working alongside Art to make sure families are cared for 24/7.

Yes, our crew is top-notch. But the thing I'm most proud of at both funeral homes is this: Every family receives great care and value. No one has to cut corners. Every family is treated with the utmost respect.

That's the legacy we've built. And that's the legacy Jon and his team continue.

So, here's a heartfelt thank you to Jon and his incredible staff—because you all make this journey worth every step.

53

FAMILY TIES AND FUNERAL TALES: THE JOYS OF A FAMILY BUSINESS

A h, the joys of running a family business. You'd think it's all warm hugs and celebratory high-fives, but let me tell you, it's more like herding cats in a thunderstorm. Family brings loyalty, history, and heart into the business—but it also brings opinions, strong personalities, and the occasional clash.

I've talked a lot about my dad, the driving force behind Thompson's Harveson & Cole (THC), and my brother Vic, the "Crown Prince"—whose charm, humor, and vision could have taken THC to new heights if life had given him more time. But our family's impact on the funeral home industry didn't stop there.

Before she ever stepped into the funeral home, my mom had a long and successful career as a chauffeur, cook, housecleaner, and general Mom-extraordinaire. And once she joined THC, she brought those same no-nonsense skills into the business.

Funeral homes sell prepaid funerals, and back in the day, the money went into a trust account that was regularly audited by the Texas Banking Commission. This thing had to be perfect to the penny, every "i" dotted and every "t" crossed.

By then, we had computers, but my mom? She trusted her spreadsheets. She might have even dusted off an abacus for all I know. The auditors were always amazed—not a single cent out of place. I'm convinced that they left THC every year wondering if my mom had supernatural powers.

My oldest sister Cindy took a detour into hospital dietary services before she joined the funeral home full-time in the early '80s. Now, my dad wasn't exactly a chauvinist, but let's be honest—back then, women weren't expected to become licensed funeral directors. It just wasn't the norm. But Cindy changed that.

After years in the business, she made the decision to get her license. That meant making the daily trek to Dallas Institute of Funeral Service, where she enjoyed better breakrooms than I had and fewer roach coaches (a major improvement, trust me). After Dad passed away, Cindy led THC with grace and grit. She proved that women belong in funeral service—and frankly, I think they often make better funeral directors than men. There's something about their natural empathy, patience, and attention to detail that sets them apart.

My sister Teacy put in years at THC before she, too, decided to get her funeral director's license. Then, she pulled the old switcheroo and swapped it for a real estate license. But once you're in the family business, it's hard to escape—no matter how many houses you sell. She put in her time, learned the ropes, and left her mark before venturing into the world of real estate.

My brother Tim took a different path—one that led straight to Rome. After high school, he entered Holy Trinity Seminary at the University of Dallas. Then, the Bishop of Fort Worth sent him to the Vatican for his final four years of study. During the summers, he worked at THC—which probably solidified his decision to stay in the seminary because let's be honest, the funeral business can push a man toward prayer.

In his third year in Rome, Tim's ordination as a Deacon was held at the Vatican itself. Naturally, we flew to Rome to be there for the occasion. We stayed at the Leonardo DaVinci Hotel, just a block from the Vatican. Tim wanted to take us to all his favorite restaurants, which meant a whole lot of walking. Now, I was expecting to eat Italian food—you know, pizza, lasagna, spaghetti. Little did I know, real Italian food was mostly fish . . . and more fish.

I kept asking, "Where's the real Italian food?" but apparently, that *was* the real Italian food. Lesson learned.

Despite the seafood overload, I can say with absolute certainty that Tim made a brilliant decision becoming a priest. He loves his church. He loves his parishes. He loves his parishioners.

I may be biased, but I truly believe he is one of the finest priests I have ever known. And yes, he's as humble as they come.

And then there's my champion, my twin sister, Martha. In my book, she's Mother of the Year—every single year. She has four daughters we lovingly call the "Mini Marthas" because they're exactly like her. She has dedicated her life to raising them, and it shows in every way.

Martha has had several stints working at the funeral home, but she spent much of her career as a schoolteacher and counselor. Through it all, she has always been my biggest champion, from the time we were toddlers to today. And now she's back working with me at THC, which just makes everything better.

In sum, running a funeral home with your family is a wild ride. It's frustrating, it's emotional, it's chaotic. But it's also deeply rewarding. I wouldn't trade these memories, experiences, or challenges for anything. Because at the end of the day, family is what keeps this business alive.

And even though we may have our differences, our arguments, and our own ideas about how things should be run—when it comes to helping families in their hardest moments, we're always on the same page.

54

THE PET PARADE

f I'm telling my life story—and let's be honest, that's precisely what this has turned into—there's no way I can leave out my pets. They've been the glue holding my sanity together, at least in my mind. Through all the ups and downs, funeral home expansions, business disasters, and triumphs, my animals have been my most loyal, nonjudgmental, and occasionally exasperating companions.

Growing up, we had **Poochie**, a ragamuffin mutt who probably predates my earliest memories. Poochie lived to chase every car or truck that dared to roll down Mistletoe Blvd. Unfortunately, one day, he finally caught one. That little adventure led to the infamous "special burial on Mistletoe."

After Poochie came **Fuzzy Wuzzy**, another mutt with a heart of gold. Fuzzy was my shadow, following me everywhere on my bicycle rides. When Fuzzy passed, my girlfriend gave me my Old English Sheepdog, **Henry**. You'll recall that Henry became my loyal companion during those lonely 9 p.m. to 7 a.m. shifts at the funeral home — until he tackled my new wife. Henry and I both learned some hard lessons that day.

When I was married to Jon's mom, I decided to up my dog game and bought an **Afghan Hound named Farah**. She was, without a doubt, the most elegant dog I ever owned. Then one of my golf buddies at Woodhaven lost his mother, leaving behind a **Shet-**

land **Sheepdog named Bogey.** I took him in, thinking I was officially a "dog person for life."

And then, I married Janice.

Janice didn't have children of her own, but she became a fantastic mom to Jon when he came to live with us—one of the greatest gifts I've ever received. And with Janice came her two dogs and a cat: **Amy,** the regal collie; **Maggie,** the mischievous beagle; and **Smokey,** the cat who ruled us all. Our friends still joke that if reincarnation exists, they want to come back as one of Janice's pets — and I don't blame them.

Smokey, my first real cat, quickly trained me in the ways of feline independence. Every morning after breakfast, she'd demand to go outside, hop our eight-foot fence, and spend the day lounging next door at Dan and Grace's. By dinnertime, she'd return home as if she'd never left. To this day, I'm not sure whose cat Smokey actually was.

When we lost Amy, Maggie, and Smokey, we rescued a gorgeous tri-color collie named **Kinzy** from a family in Weatherford. She had heartworms, and though the treatment gave her a few good years, it eventually caught up with her.

Janice believes dogs need friends (a rule she applies more strictly than most human social circles), so I went to the Humane Society and found **Charlie,** a cocker spaniel. Charlie was the most laid-back dog I've ever met — except when we drove through Dublin, Texas. Somehow, he knew when we were near the original Dr. Pepper plant. He'd get his own glass of Dr. Pepper, drink it in one go, and then let out the most impressive burp you've ever heard.

At some point, I began visiting a pet store that specialized in parrots. There was a **Blue and Gold Macaw named Emit** who had a reputation for being as mean as a snake. Every time I visited, I'd give him a walnut, and the owner would warn me, *"Careful — he'll bite."*

One day, I stuck out my hand and said, "Step up." Emit hopped right onto my finger. The owner's jaw hit the floor.

Soon, Emit came home with me, along with **Sandy the African Grey** (who mimicked my voice so perfectly that employees were constantly tricked into thinking I was answering the phone) and a temperamental **Scarlet Macaw**. For a while, my office sounded like a jungle aviary.

Eventually, as the business expanded, I had to rehome the birds. Not because I didn't love them, but because they deserved more attention than I could give.

When Charlie passed away, Janice and I adopted Winston, a Cocker Spaniel rescue. He was a red-headed ball of neuroses, but we loved him anyway.

Meanwhile, Janice's parents kept feral cats on their Brownwood ranch. One kitten decided that indoor life was more his style, and just like that, we inherited **Fred** — a cat who could be purring in your lap one second and ripping your arm off the next.

Then came **Anna Belle**, a beagle puppy I found in Grapevine. She was full of energy, much to the dismay of our other dog, **Teddy, my rescue, who** I adored, and preferred peace and quiet. Around that same time, Jon's **Jack Russell Terrier named Jack** came for a "visit" that turned into a permanent stay.

Later, we welcomed **Lola Rose**, a blue tick beagle who ruled the bed every night. Losing her was one of the hardest pet losses we've ever faced, and our hearts still ache.

Today, we share our home with **Andy**, a Moyen Poodle who technically belongs to my mother-in-law but somehow became mine, and **Harveson**, our Bernedoodle. I had high hopes Harveson would be a therapy dog at the funeral home... until he flunked training three times. I love him anyway.

When I opened Martin Thompson & Son Funeral Home, I introduced a Pet Loss option for families. I partnered with veterinarians for in-home euthanasia and worked with a pet crematory and cemetery for aftercare.

I thought it was a great idea—until I realized the families were consoling me more than I was consoling them. That was when I learned I'm better at guiding humans through grief than pets.

Looking back, we've had a parade of pets, each one leaving their paw prints on my heart. The heartbreak of losing them never gets easier, but I wouldn't trade a single moment.

The unconditional love of a pet is something truly special. Maybe that'll be the subject of my next book.

55

BANKING ON SUCCESS:
GOLF, GRIT, AND THE REAL MVP

Over the years, as you've now experienced, I've had the chance to start multiple funeral homes, and let me tell you, none of it would have been possible without some seriously great people backing me up.

The original location of Martin Thompson Funeral Home in Grapevine? That wasn't just some brilliant business move—it was possible because Janice's Aunt Connie and her parents, Myrl and Fawn (who I considered my own second parents) believed in me. They didn't just offer encouragement—they provided the financial backing that got my dream off the ground.

People often say, "It takes a village." Well, in my case, it took a very generous and understanding family.

As the business grew, so did my need for a solid banking relationship. Enter Bill Johnson and the Bank of Commerce in downtown Fort Worth. Whenever I needed something, Bill was the guy who didn't just listen—he actually said, "Yes." Having a banker who believes in you? That's like having an ace in your back pocket.

From there, my banking journey took me to Texas Bank in Grapevine, which eventually introduced me to the legendary Phil Cloud at Bank of the West. Now, Phil wasn't just some guy behind a desk. He was a true community banker—the kind who actually got to know the people he worked with. He believed in my vision, and that belief helped me push forward, even when things looked shaky. When Phil passed away, I was already back in Fort Worth, expanding again.

Now, if you ever need to make the right business connections, let me give you a little tip: get yourself a golf course membership. Some of the best business deals don't happen in boardrooms. They happen between tee boxes.

One day, while I was playing a round, a golf buddy suggested Pinnacle Bank. That's how I found Gary Noel, who has been my go-to guy these past few years. Gary and I are both nearing the end of our careers, so my hope is that he'll be my last banker. Fingers crossed.

If I'm being completely honest, though, the real MVP in this entire story isn't a banker, a business partner, or even me.

It's Janice.

Without her unwavering support over the past thirty-two years, none of this would have been possible. She's been my rock, my sounding board, and the one keeping me sane (or at least as sane as someone in the funeral business can be). Through every high and low, every risk and reward, every crazy new business venture, Janice has stood beside me.

And let's be real—I'm not always the easiest person to stand beside.

But she's done it anyway.

So, while I may have had great bankers, brilliant mentors, and supportive friends, the truth is, there's no success story without Janice.

56

GOLF, GIGGLES,
AND KEEPING SECRETS

Thanks to my incredible staff and a wife who truly understands the sacred art of the well-timed tee-off, I've managed to sneak in a bit more golf with a great group of guys over at Ridglea. We call ourselves the Rubin Group, which sounds way more official than it actually is—think less secret society, more social club with a golf addiction.

Barry's crew has a game going almost every day, and I join them whenever I can—at least once a week, sometimes more if the funeral gods are feeling generous. And then there are the almost-nightly gatherings at the South Course, where I join the guys for a drink or two and a whole lot of ribbing. You know that saying, "If you can't stand the heat, stay out of the kitchen"? Well, this kitchen is hotter than a fire at the Ridglea men's grill. Oh wait—we've actually had two of those this year. Coincidence? I think not.

I've also become a decent domino player, at least in my own mind. The guys were kind enough to give me lessons, which basically involved them saying, "Sit down, we'll teach you," and then proceeding to empty my wallet one game at a time. Consider the losses as tuition fees in the School of Hard Blocks.

As for my golf swing, well . . . it's still as unorthodox as a pink flamingo attempting to ride a unicycle, but somehow, I've been playing some of the best golf of my life. And when I inevitably shank a shot into the next county, I just smile and think, "Well, at least I don't have to make a living doing this."

Looking back, I realize just how fortunate I've been to have great friends throughout my life.

It all started with Jimmy Suarez back in first grade. I ran into Jimmy the other day, and we took a stroll down memory lane. He told me he had just sold his bar on 7th Street, The Abbey Pub. The hilarious part? Jimmy and his wife don't drink. That's like a vegan running a steakhouse—and making a killing at it.

Many of my Boy Scout buddies are still close friends. One of them, Phil Shaw, even married my twin, Martha. Talk about keeping it in the family. Then there's Chris, who's had a tremendously successful career in the medical field, running companies all over the US. He and his wife recently built a spectacular home in the Hill Country with stunning panoramic views. I'm convinced they're trying to give the Grand Canyon a run for its money.

And then there's Griff, my partner-in-crime for every member-member tournament I can rope him into. We try to play once a week. Griff has had a successful career in banking and lives in a seriously cool house on Eagle Mountain Lake. But why stop at one lakeside abode when you can buy the house next door for parties? Officially, he bought it so his parents would have a place to stay if they ever needed care. Unofficially? It's the ultimate man cave.

Griff's dad passed away a few years ago, and I was honored to be part of that service. He's buried at the historic Oakwood Cemetery, overlooking downtown Fort Worth. Griff placed a golf ball on a tee in front of his marker, and every time I have a funeral at Oakwood, I make sure it's perfectly teed up. His mom, Mrs. G, just celebrated her one hundredth birthday and still lives independently at her home on Eagle Mountain Lake. She's sharper than most people half her age and twice as much fun.

Then there's Clayne, or CD, as we call him. He followed a girl to Michigan—a girl who could easily pass for Christie Brinkley's twin sister. Honestly, I would've followed her too. Clayne stayed in funeral service, and since Michigan requires a four-year degree, he went back to school and nailed it. He eventually became the chair of the Anatomical Department at the University of Michigan. Not too shabby for a guy from Texas. Inspired by what I was doing with Martin Thompson & Son, Clayne and his family opened Fraser Family Funeral Home, offering low-cost funerals and cremations just outside Detroit. I couldn't be prouder of him and his family for carrying the torch and serving their community.

My Grapevine guys, Ron Stacy and Ronny Nordling, are still integral parts of my life, and we hit the links together whenever schedules allow. Ronny and I will be playing in October in a two-day Ambucs tournament that we've been partners in for many years. We've never won it, but Puff and I did once, proving that miracles do happen. This year marks my twenty-fifth time playing in that tournament, which is really more of a boys weekend filled with golf, poker, dominos, and jokes that should probably never see the light of day. In other words, it's perfection.

All in all, it's been an incredible ride, and I'm nowhere near ready to utter the words I did when I graduated high school: "The party's over." Quite the opposite—I'm having too much fun to stop now.

When I began writing this little project, I had no idea where it would lead. Initially, I thought about sharing some of the wild stories I've accumulated over the years in the funeral business. Trust me, there are plenty, and friends have been urging me to put them down on paper for ages. But as I wrote, I realized that some stories are better left untold, out of respect for the families who have entrusted me during their most private moments. I take that trust very seriously, so those tales will stay buried.

I also contemplated delving into some of the tougher times I've faced, but let's be honest—who wants to read a sob story when you can have a laugh instead?

In the end, I wanted this project to be a fun, quirky look at my life—with all its twists and turns. Writing it has been as much for me as it has for you, the reader. I hope I haven't bored you too much along the way.

I recently finished reading Dan Brown's *Origin*, and it's given me a glimpse into where we're headed—both in life and in our industry.

It's comforting to know that Jon will be the one steering the ship into the future, and I can't wait to see where he takes it.

As for me, I'll keep working because I love what I do—

But Jon, don't expect me to be clocking in at ninety. This time, I'm not starting over—I'm finishing strong.

CONCLUSION

Well, folks, here we are at the end of *Funeral Begins with Fun!* If you've made it this far, I'm either doing something right, or you're just really determined to finish what you start. In that case, congratulations—you've got more willpower than most people at an all-you-can-eat buffet.

As we prepare to close the lid on this book (pun absolutely intended), I hope you've found the journey as entertaining as I have. From the wild adventures of running a funeral home to the not-so-glamorous tales of commuting, pet mishaps, and the occasional ghost story, it's been a ride filled with laughter, lessons, and maybe a little bit of lunacy.

And let's be honest—if you can't find a little humor in life's everyday absurdities, you're missing out on one of its greatest gifts.

I've shared a lot about my life—probably more than my family would have preferred (sorry, y'all), but hey, that's the price they pay for having a storyteller in the family. And while I may have taken a few detours, cracked a few jokes, and gotten sidetracked along the way, I hope you've seen the heart behind it all.

Life is full of ups and downs—sometimes you're the hearse driver, sometimes you're the guy stuck behind the hearse in rush-hour traffic. Either way, it's the stories we tell, the laughs we share, and the memories we make that really matter.

So, what's the moral of all these tales?

It's simple: Don't take life too seriously.

Whether you're dealing with a two-hour commute, a misbehaving parrot, or a funeral home renovation that feels like it'll never end, remember to laugh. Because at the end of the day, life's too short not to enjoy the ride—even if that ride involves a few unexpected bumps and the occasional parking ticket.

ACKNOWLEDGMENTS

First and foremost, to my wife, Janice, and my son, Jon—you are the foundation of everything good in my life. Your love, patience, and unwavering support made all of this possible. I am forever grateful. And I should also add her parents Fawn and Myrl Furry and Aunt Connie; without them none of it would have been possible.

To my parents Guy and Kathleen Thompson, my dad the finest director period and my mom whose faith was and is and inspiration.

To my siblings, Lucinda Jane (Cindy), Victor Guy (Vic), Anne Therese (Teacy), David Timothy (Tim) and Martha Mary (Martha) I know I was a pain most of the time but it was fun.

To Jimmy Suarez and his dad, who introduced me to a lifelong love of golf;

To Griffin Gunter and his parents, who welcomed me into their family and helped shape my early years;

To Chris Guinn and his family, whose friendship and humor made the journey lighter;

To Clayne Fraser, my partner-in-crime, co-pilot, and source of endless stories;

And to Eddie Robinson, whose spirit and loyalty still guide me today.

To my Grapevine bunch—Phil Cloud, Ron Stacy, Ronny Nordling, and the many movers and shakers who believed in me and helped me build a dream.

To my bankers (you know who you are), The Rubin Group at Ridglea, and everyone I've ever played golf with, served as a funeral director, or told a joke to—thank you for adding your own chapters to my story.

To the Catholic Church, and to the priests and nuns who served with true servant hearts, doing their best to educate a stubborn kid and instill a little religion and a lot of discipline. You made a difference more than you know.

To all of the pastors and church leaders who have believed in me and allowed me to be a part of serving their church families.

To the hospice workers who make the end-of-life journey something special for families we have served and passed along a good word about our service.

To my professors at Texas Wesleyan College—especially Dr. Donnelly and Dr. Fleming—who helped me finally flip the switch and learn how to learn. Your patience and belief in me changed the course of my life.

And to my fellow funeral directors across the country who dedicate their lives to one of the most sacred, humbling services there is—I am proud to stand among you.

Each of you, in your own way, helped build this life and this book. I couldn't have done it without you.

Thank you—for everything.

ABOUT THE AUTHOR

Martin Thompson was born on April Fools' Day in Fort Worth, Texas, a fitting start for a man whose life has been full of humor, heart, and hard work.

Raised in a bustling Catholic family, Martin found his way into funeral service early, helping his father at Harveson & Cole Funeral Home and leading backyard funerals for every bird, squirrel, and pet within six city blocks. It was clear from the start that caring for others—and telling a good story about it—was in his blood.

Over the course of nearly fifty years, Martin built a career as a respected funeral director, mentor, and business owner, founding Martin Thompson Funeral Home in Grapevine, Lucas & Thompson Funeral Home in Keller, and Martin Thompson & Son Funeral Home in Fort Worth, and later returning to steward the historic Thompson's Harveson & Cole. Through it all, he earned a reputation not only for his professionalism and compassion, but for finding humor and humanity in even the most solemn moments.

Martin's life outside of funeral service is equally rich: a lifelong golfer, a proud Eagle Scout, a loyal friend, a spirited storyteller, and—above all—a devoted husband to his wife Janice, and a proud father to his son Jon.

Martin's writing is a tribute to the families he served, the friends he traveled with, and the wild, wonderful journey that turned a kid from Fort Worth into a keeper of life's most precious stories.

Today, Martin can usually be found swapping stories over coffee or an adult beverage, cheering for the TCU Horned Frogs and Texas Longhorns, chasing the perfect golf swing, or simply appreciating the rich, unpredictable humor of life, one chapter at a time.